Total Compensation:
A Practical Guide to Federal Employee Benefits

BRIAN PATRICK KUHN, CFP®

Copyright © 2013 Brian Patrick Kuhn, CFP®
All rights reserved.
ISBN: 0615779123
ISBN 13: 9780615779126

Table of Contents

Chapter 1: Introduction 1

Chapter 2: CSRS/FERS Pension 11

Chapter 3: Thrift Savings Plan (TSP) 21

Chapter 4: Long-Term Care (FLTCIP) 43

Chapter 5: Social Security 63

Chapter 6: Health Insurance (FEHB) 91

Chapter 7: Life Insurance (FEGLI) 109

Chapter 8: Job Security, Wages, Leave, and Other Benefits ... 125

Chapter 9: Working Toward Your Goals 135

About the Author

Brian Kuhn is a family wealth advisor with Planning Solutions Group, LLC. With 12 years in the financial planning field, he works with families and individuals, with a specific focus on government employees, in the areas of retirement planning, wealth preservation, and insurance protection. He is a CERTIFIED FINANCIAL PLANNER™ (CFP®), Chartered Life Underwriter (CLU®), and certified in long term care (CLTC). He also holds his FINRA Series 7, and 66 registrations. Brian graduated from Towson University with a B.S. in Business Administration.

He lives with his wife Merin and their daughter Charlotte in Odenton, MD.

"Securities offered through Triad Advisors, Member FINRA / SIPC. Advisory Services offered through Planning Solutions Group, LLC. Planning Solutions Group, LLC is not affiliated with Triad Advisors."

1
CHAPTER

Introduction

The U.S. Bureau of Labor Statistics in 2010 reported that approximately two million people work for the United States federal government, not including those employed by the postal service or the military. The United States government is by far our country's largest employer and provides extensive employee benefits. As a financial planner, I work with these benefits every day to help people reach their financial and retirement goals. Just as often I work with people who have spent their career in the private sector.

What is becoming more obvious in today's economy is the distinction between the haves and the have-nots in these two groups. Sometimes federal employees and I will be talking and they will say, "Yeah I receive accrued leave, and a pension, and so on, but I just wish they'd write me a bigger check each month and I'll take care of my own money management." If you are a federal employee, you will see in the chapters that follow that they do write you a larger check. And depending on how you use these benefits, much larger!

The two-pronged goal of this book is:

- To show federal employees that the wealth of benefits that comes from their hard-earned efforts as civil servants creates tremendous opportunities for achieving personal financial goals in collaboration with the right professionals.
- To show those in the private sector that they can still accomplish all they wish for their family and for retirement, using tools created in the marketplace and having good help Specifically there are sections entitled, "What to do for the rest of us".

For both groups of readers, knowledge, along with good communication, is power. This introductory chapter will walk through many of the goals people have as they go through their lives. These are not necessarily all financial goals but the common endeavors to which families strive. Whether you are a federal employee or in the private sector, human nature is consistent in all of us. The key, then, is how to accomplish our goals. That is where planning comes in. It doesn't always have to be financial planning, because number- crunching doesn't solve everything. As long as there is an open mind and forum for discussion, our lives can be everything we want them to be.

Retirement Goals

If you find yourself in the employ of the federal government of the United States—even a newer employee and not necessarily someone who has been there 30 years—you have situated yourself in the best financial and retirement environment money can buy. How do I know this? Well, when you work long enough as a financial planner to help people manage their money, certain patterns tend to reveal themselves. People come into the office and lay the last few decades of their financial sweat equity out on my desk and tell me they want to accomplish x, y, and z, and ask how long it will take to do so. Typically, these goals consist of the same few things. Every once in a while there are some outliers with dreams of starting a bed and breakfast someplace outside of town, or people who love their job so much they would never think of retiring, or those who have no idea what they want out of life. Usually, however, the goals consist of doing one or more of the following things:

- Retire
- Decide what to do with the house
- Travel — and then more travel
- Conserve wealth
- Help the children
- Spend time with the grandchildren
- Protect your spouse or significant other

Retire

This can take a few forms. Sometimes there is a transition to part-time consultant for a few years. Maybe retirement was just on the horizon, but a project comes up and keeps you employed part-time. Sometimes people stop working the very day they're eligible to retire. Most times, however, when people retire comes down to the income. Is there enough money coming in from Social Security, pensions, rental properties, investments, or annuities to cover the expenses?

Retirement is the transitioning from the accumulation stage to the distribution stage of life. To the extent that all the expenses can be covered by sources other than distributions from assets, or just the income those assets can provide rather than selling principal, the more successful a retirement you will have. Because it's not an asset that requires your constant attention, that demands investment discipline, or that can be broken by your emotional involvement, a pension is the perfect vehicle to cover your expenses during retirement. In Chapter 4, I'll explain just how valuable in dollar terms these pensions are.

Decide What to Do with the House

Should you pay off the house and stay, or downsize to the coast like your buddy did? He seems to be enjoying the golf courses there, right? But if the old place was kept, it could be fixed up the way you always wanted it. Some people take a line of credit out on their property to accomplish this and keep the loan throughout retirement. I'm often asked whether it's better to pay off the mortgage prior to retirement or carry it with you for the tax deduction. You can successfully retire either way; it's all about having adequate cash flow to cover your expenses. If you make it a goal to pay off the mortgage by the time retirement comes around, you can develop a plan to do it. When you first sign up for that 30-year contract, 30 years seem like a lifetime. And in the early years not very much goes to the principal, so you need patience and cash flow stability. As I'll discuss in Chapter 8, "Job Security, Wages, Leave, and Other Benefits," the job security and lifelong employment that the federal government provides, at least statistically more than the private sector, allows for this stability.

Travel, and Then More Travel

This one needs to be stressed. And folks if you think your spouse doesn't have this on their to-do list, there's a kitchen table discussion in your future. Or you could be the one who wants to get away a few times a year to various destinations. Either way, if retirement was well-planned, you're getting out of the house a few times a year.

The key to travel is that it's a onetime expense. It's not something that you can turn into a monthly bill without some willpower on your budgeting. Either that or take a trip each and every month! What happens, though, if all your retirement savings are in traditional IRA accounts or 401(k)s? It means withdrawals are taxable, no matter how sunny the location is you're taking the money out to travel to. In the course of your planning, talk to your planner about the goals of what you will spend the money on in retirement. When there are specific expenses that are one-time events, it may make sense to accumulate this sum in after-tax accounts so that when it's needed all at once it doesn't affect your overall tax picture.

Here's another consideration: Make a deal with your financial planner that everything you accumulate in your Roth IRA can be used for travel. I bet that will motivate you to make those $5,500 or $6,500 annual contributions! This strategy may make sense because, as great as the Roth IRA is, it's difficult to accumulate a large balance in it. Unless you do large conversions from your traditional IRAs, which can get expensive, the only way to build up funds in this type of account is through these annual contributions, unless your employer offers a Roth 401(k), which we will discuss later. You may not end up needing all the funds in your Roth for travel, and you may decide it's better to defer withdrawals from the Roth for as long as possible to give it a chance to grow. However if it keeps you focused on saving money for retirement, you have a better chance of succeeding.

Conserve Wealth

It's always nice to live off the yield of your money rather than the money itself. Conserving wealth is becoming more complex in this day and age. It can get eaten away by health insurance, the health-related expenses this insurance doesn't cover, a disability, retirement expenses, a volatile market, the needs of a survivor to continue with the same lifestyle, college expenses, and so on.

It's important to have discussions about these things with a planner, and it's important to constantly monitor the threat each of these things poses to your household's financial health. Among these, though, a long-term health event like Alzheimer's disease, the costs of hospital care not typically covered by health insurance, and the cost of dying by the breadwinner or recipient of a pension represent three eventualities that require the most vigilance from a planner.

Chapters 3, 6, and 7 outline the options available to federal employees for protecting against these risks. Long-term care insurance, health insurance including vision, dental and FSA plans, and life insurance are offered as options payable through payroll deduction. You never know how things will work out, but you can plan accordingly. After all, the chance of poor health late in life is why they came up with this crazy idea of retirement in the first place. What happens if you work all these years and then right as you punch out for the last time and get your gold watch you check out completely? Or worse, you can't go do all the wonderful things you had planned to do.

Take Care of Mom and Dad

The baby boom generation is turning into the sandwich generation. Their children are having a harder time finding the foothold of a good stable career and their parents are living longer than they ever thought possible. All of this is happening right at the time that they are trying for that final push of putting money away for their own retirement. This means one thing: multiple demands for scarce resources. There are checks to write for the food and shelter that junior needs while living at home a little longer. There are checks for prescriptions for Mom and maybe even a portion of a facility she lives in. There's no magic to getting through these events, just patience, love, and money.

Help the Children

I will work with clients, and it is interesting to see how sometimes their views toward their children change over time. Initially, perhaps, we get together while they are in their fifties, they're saving everything they can for retirement, and they plan to use it all once they get to where they're living the life of their dreams. "The kids? They can fend for themselves when I go."

Introduction

Then a few years go by and it's looking like this retirement thing is really going to happen. They've accumulated some money, mapped out an income plan, and maybe had a grandchild or two. Things start to change a little bit. "All right, well, hopefully there's some money left over, but I don't want them to get it all at once, they still might blow it on a car or something. He has a good job now, anyway. I'd really want them to get it over time as they grow or even better, just give it directly to grandkids. They are going to have a harder time retiring with the way this country's going."

Sound familiar? This causes us to start talking about how a living or an irrevocable trust can help put into motion this control beyond the grave that these clients desire. I'm not an attorney, so I don't draft legal documents, but any good financial planner you work with should be familiar with how trust documents affect your assets and the incredible value they can provide. We work closely with an attorney group to ensure people's wishes are carried out beyond their death.

Now here's the best part. Once we've done the planning, the trips have been taken, the house has been paid off, and the kids have grown up a little more, clients realize just how great that pension they're receiving really is. In this day and age, their children aren't going to receive that pension. They have to save for retirement on their own and usually have to do it with the stock market the way it is these days. Not too easy.

Working with my retired client at this point, I'll often get the call about withdrawals from the account. I'll say, "All right, we'll get the check out to you—everything all right?" And they'll say, "Yeah. I just figured I might not really need all this money and my kids aren't going to have this federal pension like I have, and who knows what's going to happen with Social Security, so maybe I'll help them out a little bit. Might as well help them while I can see them benefit from it." This scenario is possible only if the cash flow needs of the client and their surviving spouse are covered for their whole life regardless of what the market is doing and regardless of inflation. If you have a pension that adjusts each year and provides for income for both lives, you have a huge ace in the hole to taking care of these concerns.

Spend Time with the Grandchildren

This is most people's personal favorite retirement goal. It's rewarding, and in many cases it's free if you live close by. This sometimes isn't a goal that actually occurs during retirement. Sometimes the client loves what they do and works well into their sixties or early seventies, or they have grandchildren early and are still wrapping up their working career. The key to this is the flexibility to takes days as you need them to not miss the soccer games and recitals. As we will talk about in Chapter 8, "Job Security, Wages, Leave, and Cost of Benefits," with the federal governments leave programs it's possible to accrue over a year's worth of days to take any time there's an event or grandma and grandpa are needed for some babysitting. And if you don't end up using it all, you get a check as you're walking out the door for the last time that can take care of some last-minute debts heading into retirement. Or in the case of sick leave that is left over it gets rolled into your pension to get additional lifetime income. If you're one of the millions of people who work for small employers where leave is more difficult to come by, this isn't an option.

Protect Your Spouse or Significant Other

Sometimes it takes a financial planner to point it out in black and white, but in most cases a surviving spouse would be in rough shape if the other spouse's death occurred earlier than expected. This can be a retirement income goal or a more pronounced concern during the working years. Chapter 7, "FEGLI/Life Insurance," talks about the basic and optional coverage offered through the FEGLI (Federal Employees' Group Life Insurance) program. This program allows workers to obtain significant amounts of life insurance, up to five times the employee's salary or more, without having to go through medical underwriting, provided you sign up when you are hired.

Introduction

This Book's Goals

These goals represent some typical concerns for clients I will work with as they approach retirement, experience this wonderful time in their lives, and then start to look back over a life's work. There are others as well, and as a planner, helping people accomplish whatever it is they want out of life is what gets me out of bed in the morning. There's nothing better than getting emails from clients with completed bucket lists and "Hello from the Mediterranean" pictures. With the 78 million baby boomers heading full-speed ahead toward this age in their lives, many times what separates them from weekends at the office or weekdays at the beach is the job security, income, employee benefits, pension, and qualified retirement savings that come with a big reliable employer like the federal government. As we go through this book I hope to use case studies, statistics, tips and tricks, and my personal perspective to accomplish two things:

- First, for those readers who are part of the federal system, I hope to provide an educational refresher and appreciation for the opportunities you have been provided. You work hard for the benefits. Now let's get the most out of them.
- Second, for those readers who are in the private sector, those hopefully receiving that "larger" check in place of workplace benefits, let's recreate those federal benefits for you so that you can have the retirement of your dreams. Or in many cases the benefits available in the private marketplace, offered by thorough and independent planners offer increased flexibility and opportunities.

Despite all the doom and gloom out there in our economy and this transition to an "independent contractor" world, with a little planning and some hard work you can accomplish almost anything you want out of life.

In the chapters that follow, this book will discuss the benefits that federal workers enjoy: Thrift Savings Plan (TSP), Long-Term Care, Social Security, FERS/CSRS Pension, Health Insurance,

FEGLI/Life Insurance, and Job Security, Wages, Leave, and Other Benefits. Each chapter will have a section, "What to Do for the Rest of Us," which will present details for those who are private-sector employees.

2
CHAPTER

CSRS/FERS Pension

Let's take a look at John and Charlotte. They both work for the federal government and now are looking at retirement and want to figure out how they are doing. As we sit down to run the numbers, they tell me that they have three primary concerns. They are uncertain about how things look in general, they have lots of questions, and they fear that the money they've saved is not nearly enough.

This chapter discusses a fictional couple, two individuals who both worked for the federal government for many years, in order to demonstrate how their respective pensions help them accomplish their goals as they got older. There are frequent news stories lately about pensions going away. As for now, though, at least for federal employees they are still here. They may not always be this large, because there have been many adjustments to the programs, and that will continue as agency leaders do what's necessary to fulfill their promises to retain retirement programs. Let's hope so, anyway. If you don't have a pension, the goal is still the same—secure, reliable income to replace your daily (and at sometimes nightly) efforts at your career. Some illustrations are offered here of how to do this, but it's important to work with a financial planner so that you can be aware of all your options and use the ones that suit your tolerance and preferences.

John is 57 and has worked as an engineer for the federal government for 31 years. He just always got out of bed in the morning and went to work. He bounced around a little between agencies but started in the government when he was young because that's who was hiring. He never really thought about retirement until he got into his early fifties, because his kids started to have jobs of their own, which was great, and because his back started to act up.

He's covered under the Civil Service Retirement System (CSRS) because he started working for the federal government prior to January 1, 1984. They later offered him the opportunity to change over to the Federal Employees Retirement System (FERS) system and invest, with a match, to the TSP (Thrift Savings Plan), but he never was into the stock market, or change, so he stayed in the old plan.

Charlotte is 59 and has worked for the Department of Education for 27 years. She feels old because she's turning 60 soon and would really like to just spend time with her new grandbaby from their oldest child, who's been out of college for a few years. "John can work all he wants to, the more the better. It will keep him out of the house," Charlotte says. She's in the CSRS program as well. There was a stretch of time where she considered going into the private sector because of some shake-ups that were rumored at the department, but she stayed and things worked out.

John and Charlotte each make around $100,000 a year. It sure doesn't seem like it, though, as they are not at all close to paying off the house, even after a number of years applying extra to the principal. They are also paying a lot in taxes, and their youngest child is almost finished with college. Their monthly cash flow looks like this:

CSRS/FERS Pension

Monthly Income

John's Salary	$8,333
Charlotte's Salary	$8,333
Total	$16,666

Monthly Expenses

Income Taxes	$5,000 (30% effective rate between federal & state)
Savings (TSP & mutual fund)	$1,500
Mortgage	$4,000 ($2,500 payment and $1,500 extra)
Health/Life Insurance	$1,000
Food/Electric/Misc.	$2,000
College Costs	$2,000
Discretionary	*$1,166*
	$16,666

During the course of a given month they don't really feel like their cash flow is very good. They have a little discretionary income, but it ends up going toward car repair, college textbooks, a leaky roof, and so on. They are saving for retirement, though, but they don't get a match on these contributions because of their type of employment. They also don't receive Social Security.

We sit down to talk and decide that in one year's time the last child will be graduating college. There will still be about $100,000 left on the house by then despite the extra payments, but their plan is to sell it and pay cash for a place in North Carolina. It looks like one of their children will settle there, and they've always liked the climate. They expect their house to sell for $500,000, after dropping from $600,000 in the downturn in the economy.

Due to the savings in their TSP plan over time, they have about $200,000 combined and want to know what they can draw from that in retirement.

However, the first step here is to take a look at the pension estimates John has 31 years in, so even though he's younger than 60 his calculation puts him at an annuity income of $65,000 annually with cost of living adjustments for life and a 50% survivorship provision if he dies. By 50% it means upon John's death the annuity would continue to Charlotte however be cut in half. Charlotte will be 60 by the time she starts her payment, also with inflation adjustments and survivorship, and with 27 years will receive $60,000. I walk them through the following breakdown of monthly income and expenses.

Monthly Income

John's Pension	$5,416
Charlotte's Pension	$5,000
Total	$10,416

Monthly Expenses

Income Taxes	$3,124 (30% effective rate between federal & state
Property Taxes on NC	$500
Health/Life Ins.	$600
Food/Electric/Misc.	$1,500
Discretionary	**$4,692**
Total	$10,416

So without accessing any of the retirement investments they have accumulated or completely paying off the house they spent most of their working years in, John and Charlotte can look forward to approximately $4,500 every month in income that is entirely discretionary. They are both healthy overall, and with Charlotte only 60 years old, they can reasonably expect another 20 years of life.

They live in a low cost-of-living suburban area, and their pension income will automatically rise with inflation for the rest of their lives. Inflation is tracked through a government monitored calculation called the CPI/W or Consumer Price Index for Urban Wage Earners and Clerical Workers. If either one of them passes away, the survivor can rely on a combined income of approximately $100,000 and growing from that point forward. Cost-of-living adjustments may not come every year or be a substantial percentage given the low inflation period currently but will adjust if necessary.

Consider for a moment what life would look like if John and Charlotte worked in the private sector for these same time periods and had accumulated the same retirement savings. They would receive Social Security but couldn't begin taking payments until age 62. If both of them initiated payments at that age it would be a reduced payment from their full benefit, so let's say $1,500 a month each. They would need to draw on their 401(k) plan of $200,000 and perhaps allocate it to a fixed income and dividend portfolio paying out 5% or $10,000. This is by no means guaranteed, nor is it scheduled automatically to increase substantially over time. That puts their retirement income at $3,833 total before taxes and the other expenses listed above. Additionally, if either were to pass away, one of the Social Security payments would stop, as will be explained in Chapter 5, "Social Security," leaving only approximately $2,400 a month for the survivor.

Now you might say if they had worked in the private sector for their whole career they would be aware of the increased need for retirement savings so would have accumulated more than $200,000. Well, tell that to the millions of workers today who, despite as much sweat equity as one body can handle over 30 plus years, haven't even accumulated the $200,000 listed here due to family needs or layoffs, or health expenses, and market downturns.

The discretionary income John and Charlotte receive each month will make a difference in the lives of every generation to follow them, through accumulated investments during retirement, opportunities with life insurance, and college funding for grandchildren and great-grandchildren. The options are endless.

How Federal Pensions Are Calculated

The CSRS was started in 1920 and over the years has covered millions of retirees. The CSRS pension is computed by taking 1.5% of your "high-3" average pay times service up to five years plus 1.75% of your "high-3" for years 5 through 10, and 2% of your "high-3" for all years after 10. "High-3" means the highest three years of earnings. This calculation does not take into account if you retire prior to age 55, include any sick leave that is eligible to be added in, or take into account if there is a disability. So if the three years that you made the most income at the government were $80,000, $82,000, and $84,000, then the average would be $82,000. They would take 1.5% of that figure or $1,230 times 5, which is $6,150. Then they would add $82,000 times 1.75% multiplied by 5 or $7,175. Then, if you worked for 30 years total, it would also add 20 at 2% for a total of $32,800. The sum of all these is $46,125. If you are a CSRS employee, check with your human resources area for unique characteristics about how your payment is being calculated and for an estimate based on your work record. Check this calculation for accuracy over time and work with a wealth advisor to assess how the income stream will be incorporated into an overall plan.

On January 1, 1984, the federal government started the transition from the CSRS system to what's called the FERS system or Federal Employee Retirement System. You can probably guess the answer here, but now that you know just how big some of the pensions can be for a typical employee, do you think they adjusted the benefit up or down? In the FERS computation, it works as follows. The worker fully entitled to a pension would take 1% of the same high three average years and multiply it by the number of years of service. Given the same data as above, it would be 1% of $82,000, or $820 multiplied by 30 or $24,600 annually. As you can see, this represents a noticeable reduction from the $46,125 figure above. Now in exchange for this reduced calculation, the FERS recipient did receive an additional benefit. As Chapter 3, "Thrift Savings Plan (TSP)," will outline, the employee can participate in the Thrift Savings Plan to defer taxable income for retirement but will also receive a match on those contributions. FERS participants are also eligible to participate fully in Social Security.

FERS employees have an extra supplement that assists them in their transition to retirement. It's called the special retirement supplement or SRS. Employees who qualify and retire prior to age 62 will receive an extra annuity payment that is meant to account for what Social Security would provide if the retiree were of age. It stops at age 62 as they are eligible to begin Social Security payments. To qualify one must either have 30 years of service and have reached their minimum retirement age, or have 20 years of service and be age 60 or older.

What to Do for the Rest of Us

The federal pension is an annuity. The definition of an annuity is a series of payments guaranteed to last a specified period of time. In this case, the period would be the annuitant's life, almost always with a survivorship provision for the spouse. This provides an income stream during retirement that a household can count on to cover a certain amount or all of their expenses each month. This is a structured way toward successful retirement living. If the bills are paid regardless of how the investment assets are doing, or what the house is worth, cash flow will always be positive.

If you don't have a pension, what are you to do? There needs to be income from the assets you have set aside for this period of your life. It can come in many forms. You can own properties where you receive rent, or own stocks that are paying dividends. As a stockholder, you are entitled to a share of the company's earnings if they choose to pay them out in the form of a dividend.

Similarly, a bond portfolio could be created that pays interest each month. As a bondholder, you are receiving interest on funds you have lent the entity. Bonds may be issued by corporations investing in new technology, municipalities expanding, or the federal government. It could even be foreign governments borrowing funds for growth, and they all pay interest that individuals can use for living expenses. Some plans actually will involve investing for growth over time using these vehicles and selling a portion of them periodically to use for cash flow, in addition to the interest or dividends they provide.

Another increasingly popular method of structuring an income stream for retirement is to buy an annuity. Now, investing in an annuity can frankly be a daunting task. There are as many opinions about whether they deserve a place in your financial plan as the day is long.

There are many terms and types of annuities to consider, most of which are beyond the scope of this book. Some general concepts, however, deserve explanation here to give you an idea of what to look for. Before we discuss them, though, remember the assets of John and Charlotte. John, again, was entitled to an annuity payment starting at age 58 with 55% survivorship for Charlotte. One form of annuity is called a SPIA or Single Premium Immediate Annuity. Single premium means just one deposit as opposed to a series of payments. Immediate means the payment would begin immediately or within one year.

Using a vehicle like this for comparison, we could calculate approximately how much John and Charlotte would need to deposit to recreate this annuity had they not worked for the government. Using a large, highly rated insurance company, the deposit required to obtain a lifetime payment of $65,000 annually for a 58-year-old, with a 50% survivorship guaranteed for their 60-year-old spouse, is $1,980,000.00! This also is only a level payment, meaning it will never increase, whereas the federal pension has the opportunity annually to increase with increases by the rate of inflation. That alone could add approximately $1,000,000 to this figure. This isn't meant to diminish the value of an annuity, as they are very popular vehicles to recreate this structured stream of income. It's meant to convey the sheer amount of money required to provide a federal pension.

Regarding annuities, you can invest in one with various types of assets, whether it is after-tax funds like cash or mutual funds, or an IRA through a rollover from an old employer's plan. One of the first choices here is whether you're going to use an immediate annuity or a deferred annuity. These two types simply refer to when the income will begin, whether it will start now or sometime in the future.

A deferred annuity is used most often in the marketplace today based on the fact that in many cases the income is intended to begin years in the future. Within deferred annuities there are fixed, variable, hybrid, and indexed. These all have unique features that should be thoroughly explained by a competent professional. There is one feature, however, that is common enough these days to mention. It used to be, many years ago, that if someone purchased an annuity, when it came time for the income to begin there would be a process called annuitization. This means the funds in the contract would be used to purchase an irrevocable payment for a specified period of time, just like the textbook definition we discussed. This caused the owner of the annuity to lose control of the funds in exchange for this structured payment. This may or may not be in the owner's best interest, and a recommendation either way is not prudent here, however, given that when offered the option of losing control of an asset versus not losing control most people would choose the latter. The insurance companies offering these products figured this out and have begun to offer products where an income stream can be structured for life, but the owner is not required to give up control of the investment.

This is called an optional income living benefit rider that is added to the underlying contract. The features of these riders should be thoroughly explained and understood by the prospective owner prior to purchase, and they are included in a majority of contracts today. Between a lump-sum deposit or a series of payments leading up to retirement, a household can structure an income stream that lasts a lifetime, covers both lives, even in some cases increase the payment over time.

Consider your options, especially more than one, and see if the tools in the marketplace can accomplish your goals.

CHAPTER 3

Thrift Savings Plan (TSP) & Qualified Plans

Each chapter in this book begins with a story of someone trying to achieve their financial goals. The stories are meant as an opportunity to take a step back from the number crunching and analysis and just relate to the everyday decisions people go through as they approach the rest of their lives. The people may be federal employees or they may not. It's important for all to be aware of these benefits and their effects on your peers, spouses, clients, and even our country.

    Mike worked for a software company. He got the job at age 53, and it was really the first time in his life he had the opportunity to put away any money for retirement. Prior to that it seemed something always got in the way. Either it was the car breaking down, or the company didn't offer a plan, or his daughter Julie's college education.

Now was finally his chance. The company offered a 401(k) plan with a series of investment choices, and he could allocate a portion of his savings to the company's stock. He tried to contribute the maximum he could each year; most years he got almost there, and the company offered a match on those deposits that equated to another $6,000 annually. Mike never followed the market and didn't really know how much he needed to retire. He just tried to do the best he could for his wife and family.

This chapter outlines the basics of investing. Federal employees invest through the Thrift Savings Plan (TSP), which operates similarly to a 401(k) plan. We will talk about different asset classes and tolerance for risk, and for those in the private sector, we'll look at how to save for your financial goals using the tools typically available to you.

Mike talked to a colleague at the office and set up an allocation for his contributions that included 50% equities, 30% fixed income and cash, and 20% company stock. He was grateful the company gave him the position and the extra money they put in on his behalf. He figured he could keep a closer eye on the valuation of the company than the market as a whole.

A few years went by and as he started to get closer to retirement he never really made changes to his allocation. There was never really a reason. He was always just told to ride things out. Mike got to be 62 and started thinking about retirement. Over the course of that year, however, things started to change at the company. There were firms overseas that could do the same thing for half the cost. The stock valuation started to take a turn.

He began opening his statements for the first time in a while. Before that year, he figured it didn't make a difference since he wasn't retiring yet. He opened the statement and it said $222,657.00. It seemed like a fair amount, but then he thought for a moment. "I've been putting money into this account for almost 10 years. Each year that contribution has been about $18,000 on average. The company put in $6,000 annually during that time. That's $216,000! And I only have $222,000 in my account?" The equity markets had been up and down during that time period but hadn't really developed any consistency. And the company's stock ended up going down 50%. He ran an online calculator that stated he should plan on taking 4% of his accumulated balance as an income stream in retirement. That would be $8,906. "I certainly can't afford to retire on that," Mike said. He would receive Social Security and so would his wife, but he was always told he would take a big discount if he started it now. "I'll just keep working and see if things turn around, I guess. I don't mind working, but it would be nice to know that I could stop or slow down if I needed to. I just don't hop out of bed like I used to. The income just isn't there. I hope the market comes back, but what if it doesn't?"

One leg of the three-legged retirement stool has always been savings. Employers provide these plans for employees to save on a tax-deferred basis for later. This can be a 401(k), 403(b), 457, SIMPLE IRA, or other plans. They all accomplish the same thing: providing the option for the employee to elect to lower current income by deferring it into an investment account. These contributions and their growth are taxed when distributions occur at a later date, typically as a systematic payment the employee uses to live on in retirement. The plan may not still be with the employer at that time, as most people do a rollover to an IRA or individual retirement account. These plans are effective for accumulating money for retirement, and it's generally a good idea to save as much as possible, given your budget, into the account. You can set up a broadly diversified portfolio; adjust the allocation over time based on your risk tolerance, age, and goals. The federal government offers a plan as well, called the Thrift Savings Plan (TSP).

This chapter will outline several subtle differences between the TSP and what you will typically find in the private sector. The following differences will be explained one-by-one in detail:

- A favorable vesting schedule on matching contributions to the plan and an automatic deposit by the employer whether you contribute or not. (This is for FERS employees and not CSRS which we will further discuss in the pension chapter).

- The standard election of a Traditional TSP account allowing for tax-deferred growth
- The option of an elective Roth TSP account allowing for tax-free growth
- Low-cost, passive investment funds.
- A stable, highly-funded plan that has the advantage of consistency and reliability to the participants.
- The ability to turn the accumulated balance into an annuity upon retirement (Although rarely elected).
- The option of withdrawing funds directly from the TSP without a 10% penalty once separated from service at age 55 as opposed to the usual age of 59.5 on an IRA or some employer plans.
- Timeline-based allocation funds that can take the guessing out of investment picking
- The flexibility to withdraw or take loans upon reaching age 59.5 or as necessary, respectively. Some plans do not offer either of these options.

Favorable Vesting Schedule and Automatic/Matching Contributions

In the private sector, a company retirement plan may include a match on employee contributions. For example, for every dollar you put in up to 3% of your salary, the company will match dollar for dollar. This comes with a catch, however. The money may go into the account right away, but you have to stay with the employer a certain number of years to fully "vest" in that contribution. This term can be anywhere from three to about seven years depending on the plan. In today's fast-paced economy, job changes due to downsizing, having to move for a spouse's career change, or leaving to take care of a family member can force you to leave money in the plan because you weren't fully vested. It's difficult enough to accumulate funds with market volatility and competing needs for extra cash flow, let alone having to give some

Thrift Savings Plan (TSP) & Qualified Plans

back to take another job. Let's take a look at the federal employee's employee and employer contribution table for comparison.

% of Your Salary You Contribute	Automatic Contribution %	Matching Contribution %	Total Contribution %
0	1	0	1
1	1	1	3
2	1	2	5
3	1	3	7
4	1	3.5	8.5
5	1	4	10

A few observations about this schedule and the vesting requirements: There is an automatic contribution whether the employee participates or not. It may not seem like much, but it's unlike any other defined contribution plan in the business. One of the only plans close to it is the SIMPLE IRA in the private sector, if the employer chooses the non-elective contribution of 2% of salary. With this plan and this employer election, however, there is no matching contribution. It's one or the other. The Thrift Savings Plan offers both for FERS participants. It is important for FERS employees to spread their TSP contributions over all 26 pay periods of the year to get the full government match. Consider this — if an employee does not contribute in a given pay period, the government has nothing to match.

Another helpful feature of this schedule is how much of the employee's contribution the government will match. With the economy these days, companies have reduced or even eliminated their matching contributions. Many plans will match up to around 3% of the participant's contributions, or may match 50% of the contributions up to 6%. Both of these options result in a lower total dollar amount being deposited into the plan.

And lastly is the vesting schedule. FERS employees have to be employed for three full years before they are vested in the agency contributions.

Roth TSP

In the world of financial planning there aren't too many more effective options than the Roth IRA/TSP. All an advisor has to do is mention "Tax-Free Income" and the client's eyes light up. The fundamentals are that in place of getting a tax deduction for putting the money in, like a 401(k) or traditional IRA, the investments grow tax free for retirement. The difficulty with the Roth, however, is accumulating a large enough balance to make it worthwhile in retirement. There are three ways to add money to a Roth.

The first way is to contribute to a Roth IRA. However, in 2012 the limits were $5,000 if you are under 50 and $6,000 if you are over 50. If that weren't limiting enough, there were also household income limitations that, also for 2012, cap out at $183,000. So if your income is higher than this, you're phased out from making a contribution.

Here's a tip for those beyond the income limit who are looking for methods to accumulate Roth assets. It is important to get the help of both a well-qualified planner and a tax accountant who can work together to develop a strategy for you. If your earnings are too high for a deductible IRA contribution, that doesn't mean you can't contribute, it's just that you can't deduct it when you file your taxes. So once those funds are in the IRA, what's stopping you from converting them to a Roth right away? You're right, nothing because the income limits on a conversion, explained here, have been lifted. Again, see a tax professional as you are considering this, because I, and all financial planners, cannot provide tax advice.

Even better, because the funds are not considered pre-tax, they are also not taxable at the time they are converted. You must be aware of any earnings the original contribution achieved, and there's something called the pro-rata rule to be aware of, but working with your professional contacts on this strategy may allow funds into the Roth status in a systematic, efficient manner.

The second way is a Roth conversion. This entails taking a traditional IRA, 401(k), or similar tax-deferred account and converting it into a Roth IRA. Now what happens when you do this?

Thrift Savings Plan (TSP) & Qualified Plans

It will all be taxable income in the year of the conversion. Let's say your household income is $100,000 and you want to position $100,000 of IRA funds into a Roth status, your total income for that year would be $200,000. The first $100,000 would have taxes withheld as you earned it, so there shouldn't be any big checks to write to the IRS at the end of the year. On the Roth, though, all the taxes have to be paid at once. In this scenario, even after accounting for deductions like a home mortgage, taxes may still be 25% or more, which would be approximately $25,000. Ideally, when we work with clients on Roth conversions we talk about how these taxes will be paid. We don't want the funds to come from the balance in the IRA. We want all that money to get into the Roth for tax-free growth for later. That means it has to come from available cash. The benefit for retirement is tremendous, but finding that much cash and still having enough left over for an emergency reserve can be difficult, especially in this economy. Of course you don't have to convert $100,000 in one year, and when working with clients we find that doing small amounts at a time is a popular strategy. You still have to find the cash, though, to pay the IRS, which requires discipline to set aside the funds for tax time.

This leads us to the third way: the Roth 401(k), or in this case the Roth TSP. This is arguably the best option for many of the reasons listed below. The Roth 401(k) is mostly a concept at this point because despite its inception in 2006 as part of the Pension Protection Act, it has not been widely adopted. The Roth TSP allows the federal participant to defer employment income, after paying tax, into an account that will then grow tax-free. As of 2013, participants younger than age 50 are able to contribute up to $17,500 in "regular" contributions, and if the participant is over age 50, he or she can add $5,500 in "catch-up" contributions for a total available contribution of $23,000. The participant can choose to divide their contribution in any mixture between the Roth TSP and Traditional TSP, but the maximum of $17,500 (or $23,000 if at least age 50) applies to the total contribution. At these levels it is possible to accumulate a sizable account balance for tax-free retirement income in the Roth side of TSP. Additionally; there is the automated discipline of saving through payroll deduction at work. It's important to be aware the employer contributions, whether it's the TSP or a private employer that creates a Roth option, are still taxable upon withdrawal.

Passive Investment Strategies

Investing passively entails buying assets and holding them for long periods of time regardless of the market's swings. Active management by comparison allows investment managers to monitor the market's events to buy and sell assets, like stocks and bonds, to achieve performance better than just buying and holding. There are advantages to both methods and debates occur in the industry as to the best strategy for given individual investor. For employees of the federal government a passive investment strategy is the required choice.

Thrift Savings Plan Option	Benchmark	Description of Investments	Expense Ratio
G Fund	U.S. Govt. bonds specially designed only for participants.	Interest income without risk of loss of principal	0.025%
F Fund	Barclay's Capital U.S. Aggregate Bond Index	Government, corporate, and mort-gage-backed bonds	0.025%

C Fund	Standard & Poor's 500 (S&P 500) Index	Stocks of large and medium-sized U.S. companies	0.025%
S Fund	Dow Jones U.S. Completion TSM Index	Stocks of small-to-medium-sized U.S. companies	0.024%
I Fund	Morgan Stanley Capital International EAFE Index	International stocks of 21 developed countries	0.025%

One advantage of passive investing is the expenses are lower. Take a look at the expense ratios on the right side of this chart. Private-sector investors will have a very difficult time finding expense ratios anywhere near this low. This ratio means on an investment of $100,000 in the C Fund, which invests in stocks, the federal participant will pay a grand total of $25 per year! It would be difficult to find a competent broker to manage your investments for $2 per month! To be fair to the statistics, the expense ratio on funds fluctuates annually based on forfeitures by participants who leave federal service without fully vesting in automatic or vesting contributions, explained earlier. Although over the last few years it has consistently hovered in the .02 to .04% range, it did get as high as 0.1% in 2003. So here participants would pay a total $100 annually to have their assets managed over the course of a year.

Compare that to analysis from the *2011 Investment Company Fact Book*, which outlines fees for the average stock and bond mutual fund in 2010. The average stock mutual fund had an expense ratio of .95%. This means that if you had $100,000 invested over the course of a year with the fund, you would pay $950 to have that money managed, whether you make money in the investment or not. The average bond mutual fund had a fee of .72%, which calculates to $720 per $100,000 of invested assets. Yields on bonds are at some of the lowest levels they've been in decades, and stocks have become even more volatile over the last few years, so any appreciation is that much harder to generate.

It can be done though and good managers are out there earning excellent returns for investors. In some cases you get what you pay for. They are available in the TSP however.

Highly Stable Plan

It is one thing to make enough income to be able to set some aside for retirement and ride out the movements of your investment. It is another to not be able to rely on the plan where you are saving the money. In today's fast-paced, constantly changing financial services sector, you also have to be aware of corporate decisions at the investment company that's watching your money. In the private sector, you may be invested in a mutual fund or a set of mutual funds, and without knowing it the management team of one of those funds will leave to set up their own shop. That leaves your investment in the not-necessarily-capable hands of whatever manager has been hired to take over. Not so with the TSP plan. Because an index-based passive investment approach is taken, all that needs to be done is to match the benchmark. Changes are only made as necessary to reward a stock for growing fast enough to join the list, or to sell a position that has fallen enough out of favor that it no longer participates in the index being tracked.

Plan changes cause anxiety among individual investors. In many cases large amounts of mail are delivered to participants that should be combed over for specific details of the new offering and how the changes affect a participant's specific investment choices. I've worked with people who felt overwhelmed by these mailings and as a result would suddenly lose confidence in their decision because they didn't understand what's happening to the plan or their money, despite being on a regular savings rate into the plan up until then. Sometimes the employer will, for whatever reason, choose to go with another investment company altogether, causing participants to have to choose their entire asset allocations all over again. The new plan may not allow the old account balances that participants have accumulated to be consolidated into the new plan, leaving them to keep tabs on two different account balances at once.

The table below outlines what percentage of employees in our economy today has a retirement plan through work across different sector groups. Although it represents all public-sector workers and not just federal, it's interesting to see how much higher the availability and participation is in the public sector than in the private sector. It outlines also that only 39.5% of all private-sector employees participate at all in their company-offered plans. So a large majority of workers, when counting the fact that only half have a plan in the first place, are not even saving for retirement, let alone have a pension to supplement.

Percentage of Various Work Forces That Work for an Employer That Sponsored a Retirement Plan, and the Percentage of Workers Who Participated in a Plan, 2010

	All Workers	Wage & Salary Workers Ages 21–64	Private-Sector Wage & Salary Workers Ages 21–64	Public-Sector Wage & Salary Workers Ages 21–64
Worker Category Total (Millions)	152.6 m	128.0 m	106.9 m	21.1 m
Works for an employer sponsoring a plan	75.0 m	69.4 m	52.5 m	16.9 m

Participates in that plan	60.7 m	57.4 m	42.3 m	15.2 m
Works for an employer sponsoring a plan	49.2%	54.2%	49.1%	80.3%
Participates in that plan	39.8%	44.9%	39.5%	71.9%

Source: Employee Benefit Research Institute estimates from the 2011 March Current Population Survey.

The TSP offers myriad resources and educational opportunities to participants through the following website:
http://www.tsp.gov.

The site provides historical performance information, plan announcements, qualified account rules that affect how you can access funds, and online access with fund exchange privileges. The individual fund offerings manage billions of dollars for participants. All five fund offerings, as of December 2011, included more than $325 billion in overall assets, according to the TSP Fund Information report released in July 2012.

Annuity Option Upon Retirement

At retirement, the TSP offers participants the ability to turn their account value into a lifetime annuity. This is separate from and would be in addition to their CSRS or FERS annuity. While taken only by a minority of participants as they leave work, the option gives a level of peace of mind that income can be safely generated if needed to meet monthly obligations. Moreover, people do not need to deal with the process of rolling over the funds to an IRA or finding someone they trust to handle all the logistics of creating the annuity with this option. While generally all qualified retirement accounts can be transferred to an annuity for retirement income, the ability to create one without much of the legwork can be helpful if individuals really feel it is in their best interest to annuitize.

Age 55 Provision

If federal employees choose to separate from service at age 55 or later they will not be penalized for accessing funds in their TSP account compared to the normal required age of 59.5. This can be a huge help to people who have managed to put their affairs in order at an early age and, with some proper planning, would like to retire ahead of schedule. However, it is important to note that while you may not be penalized for withdrawing money prior to 59.5, you will still be responsible for paying the taxes owed as if it were ordinary income.

Let's say you are a FERS participant and feel you are ready (and eligible) to retire at 56. However, you are not eligible for Social Security until age 62 at the earliest. Perhaps you have some Roth IRA or traditional IRA assets, but they can't be used until age 59.5 unless you meet an exception or agree to take the payments as part of what's called substantially equal periodic payments. This is a rather restrictive program beyond explanation here. All this only leaves the TSP as an available option for supplemental income. You can take a monthly amount out, pay income tax, and use these funds without any 10% penalty. If the need ends, or you decide you don't want to sell your investments due to market conditions, you can simply stop. For FERS participants there is also something called a Special Retirement Supplement or SRS which is explained in the FERS/CSRS section but this age 55 provision adds an extra layer of flexibility.

Some 401(k) plans offer this provision as well, but not everyone has a 401(k), so they may not be able to take advantage of this feature. If you have a SIMPLE IRA, SEP IRA, or are just depositing funds into a traditional IRA to save for retirement, you must wait until age 59.5 to access funds without a 10% penalty, with some exceptions (shown on the list below). These exceptions, of course, other than the substantially equal periodic payments, are not designed to provide unlimited accessibility the way the age 55 feature does.

A 10% early withdrawal penalty would not apply to a distribution from a traditional IRA in the following circumstances:

- You have unreimbursed medical expenses that are more than 7.5% of your adjusted gross income.
- The distributions are not more than the cost of your medical insurance (this is related only to a loss of employment)
- You are disabled.
- You are the beneficiary of a deceased IRA owner.
- You are receiving distributions in the form of an annuity (substantially equal periodic payments).
- The distributions are not more than your qualified higher education expenses.
- You use the distributions to buy, build, or rebuild a first home.
- The distribution is due to an IRS levy of the qualified plan.
- The distribution is a qualified reservist distribution (for those in the military reserve)

Age-based, In-service Withdrawal

Another planning technique available to federal participants is what's called an "age-based, in-service withdrawal". At age 59.5 or later, they have a one-time opportunity to move any or all of their TSP account and transfer them into a Traditional IRA even though they have not yet retired. After completing an "Age-based, In-service withdrawal," the participant (once retired) must either leave the funds within TSP without taking any distributions, or take a full withdrawal.

Contributions they are doing through payroll deduction will continue on as though no transaction occurred and will begin to accumulate again for when actual retirement occurs. This is an especially important feature for FERS participants who receive matching contributions (since there is no delay in their ability to continue to contribute, there is no loss of matching funds paid by their agency).

This type of withdrawal is particularly handy if there is a lucrative IRA opportunity or if participants would like to get the investments working for them in a different type of strategy than just the available options in TSP.

Lifecycle Funds

One of the most popular trends in financial planning today is the use of what's called lifecycle or target date retirement funds. These are popular because they are easy to explain, they take some of the guesswork out of asset allocation, and they provide broad diversification within just one mutual fund.

In the TSP plan there are 5 of these options ranging from "L Income" meaning your asset allocation is that of someone withdrawing funds now, to the "L 2020, 2030, 2040 and 2050" fund which allocates funds as though you intend to begin withdrawals in that year.

The way target date funds work whether they are the TSP or in a private sector 401(k) is to set up an asset allocation of the mutual fund company's offerings as though the buyer of that fund will retire by the future date in the title. So, for example, an investment in the "Retirement 2030" fund would allocate the money as though the buyer is planning to retire in the year 2030. The allocation today will obviously lean heavier on high-growth potential stocks, and as the person ages will automatically shift more assets into fixed-income bond investments.

The owner of the fund does not need to make sure this happens, because the investment company will rebalance the positions regularly over the years to preserve value. Although these positions are logical for the novice investor and may very well perfectly allocate a portfolio over several decades, it is important to point out that they by no means ensure the account value will grow to a level sufficient for someone to retire in 2030, and they also have no way of taking into account the personal tolerance for risk that investors may have, regardless of their ages.

The uncertain future of the global economy, inflation threats to bond prices, and sometimes the personal inability to ride out the wild swings of the markets make these funds anything but a flawless guarantee of retirement success. With that said, this is about as good as it gets for automatic asset allocation and automated rebalancing. Because the fund family is choosing the positions that will make up the overall allocation, they can choose among their fund offerings that correlate well with each other and break down the holdings among those investments they think will outperform. Let's take a look at one commonly known target date fund that's used frequently today in the private sector.

American Funds 2030 Target Date Retirement Fund® Class A Share Underlying Fund Allocation as of September 30, 2012

Growth Funds: 40.0%	
AMCAP Fund®	7.0%
EuroPacific Growth Fund®	4.0%
The Growth Fund of America®	7.0%
The New Economy Fund®	4.0%
New Perspective Fund®	7.0%
New World Fund®	4.0%
SMALLCAP World Fund®	7.0%
Growth-and-Income Funds: 35.0%	
American Mutual Fund®	6.0%
Capital World Growth and Income Fund®	5.0%
Fundamental Investors℠	6.0%
International Growth and Income Fund℠	3.0%
The Investment Company of America®	7.0%
Washington Mutual Investors Fund℠	8.0%
Equity-Income/Balanced Funds: 20.0%	
American Balanced Fund®	8.0%
Capital Income Builder®	6.0%
The Income Fund of America®	6.0%
Bond Funds: 5.0%	
U.S. Government Securities Fund®	5.0%

Source: http://www.americanfunds.com

This table shows that the individual investor will have holdings across several different industries, company sizes, countries, and bond types. Even if all of these underlying investment choices were available in the employer's retirement plan, it would be difficult to know how to assemble this breakdown of funds and subsequently maintain this allocation, and how to assemble a consistently more conservative one over time through disciplined rebalancing. So how does this table relate to government employees? To be able to invest in these types of funds, they have to be offered by the overall plan, and in the private sector, despite progress in this direction, not all retirement plans offer this all-in-one solution. Therefore, participants will be left to create their own allocation out of the offerings, and to monitor and rebalance that allocation over time. The TSP plan offers these target date funds, and participants can allocate some or all of their balance to the option of their choice.

Loans

When working with private-sector individuals, especially young households, one common objection to saving money into a retirement plan is the fear of the unknown. You may need the money prior to 59.5 and therefore incur a penalty to access the funds. You may lose the investment they are putting in and would then be in no better of a position than when they started, other than perhaps the tax deduction. You cannot forecast this 10-to-30 plus year time frame where they must part with access to the funds in exchange for an unclear future benefit. In the investment environment today it's easy to understand their concern. Let's say the person is 30–40 years old, meaning they have a 20-to-30-year time horizon. You are putting children through school, maintaining a house and vehicles, trying to accumulate a savings account, and now must set aside funds that can't be touched for multiple decades regardless of what the future holds.

There are circumstances where they can, of course, access the funds, like the list of exceptions provided by the IRS presented earlier, but these are not typically the events you want to occur.

Knowing that a substantial medical expense or a disability preventing your gainful employment in any meaningful job must occur before you may access your own funds without a penalty doesn't exactly provide peace of mind.

If you are a federal employee contributing to the TSP and find yourself in a position where funds are needed, you have the ability to request a loan from your account. Let's discuss the flexibility of the TSP's loan program. Your ability to borrow is not dependent on your credit score, or any required financial documentation (provided it's a general-purpose loan as opposed to a residential loan) on your cash flow situation. Try telling that to a local bank. Of course, these are your own funds we are talking about in the plan, but after working with hundreds of households over the years on the financial and mental endurance it takes to save for retirement, I can tell you that the capability to access funds through a loan can sometimes make the difference between success and failure.

Let me explain. If two people have the same job making the same amount of money and want the same things out of life, they will have the same concerns. They will both worry about unforeseeable expenses in the future such as hospital bills, car accidents, and so on. What if one can access funds from a retirement plan and one can't? The first might say, "Well, I'll save money into the plan because I can always access it if I need it. Hopefully, I don't, but if I do I'll pay it back and the interest on that loan goes into my account, too. So I'll start by saving $500 a month." On the other hand, the second might say, "I can only afford to put in what I know I won't need for the next several years unless something really goes wrong, so I'll put in $250 a month and try to save the other $250 after tax and put it in a savings account or mutual fund."

What happens? First, in the latter case the second $250 each month will be taxed. Next, the second individual has to successfully identify the net amount out of each paycheck and set it aside in another account before expenses and discretionary spending get the better of it. This takes discipline over a long period of time. Some people have no problem with it; others talk themselves into needing that money for something besides their future just about five minutes after it arrives into their bank account.

So what just happened here? Let's assume that over the entire investing time period of both of these individuals neither one of them needed any of these funds in the form of a loan or an unforeseen expense. Due to taxes both on the second $250 and on anything that investment makes in the form of capital gains, bond interest, or stock dividends, the second person will come out behind. Now the second individual, assuming he or she really did set the money aside each month, will have half of his retirement savings in an after-tax account rather than an account waiting to be taxed in retirement, but what I'm referring to here is the psychological difficulty of saving in our modern society. It will be easier for the first person to never see the money or pay taxes on it and know in the back of his or her mind that the money can be accessed, if necessary, than it will be for someone to recreate that level of accumulated wealth after the pressures of everyday life. That's why the concept of qualified savings plans was created.

A loan from the TSP balance is easy to request (see the following website for details):

https://www.tsp.gov/planparticipation/loans/loanBasics.shtml

There is a one-time $50 administrative fee, and the funds are received as a non-taxable lump sum. If you sever employment or default on the loan, it will become taxable and there are possible penalties. There are some items not related to one's credit score that are required in order to qualify to take loans; these are listed at the website above. Also, the maximum amount of the loan is more complex than a fixed dollar amount (see the following breakdown).

The maximum loan amount is the smallest of the following:

Your own contributions and earnings on those contributions in the TSP account from which you intend to borrow, not including any outstanding loan balance; or 50% of your vested account balance (including any outstanding loan balance) or $10,000, whichever is greater, minus any outstanding loan balance; or $50,000 minus your highest outstanding loan balance, if any, during the last 12 months. Even if the loan is currently paid in full, it will still be considered in the calculation if it was open at any time during the last 12 months.

Source: http://www.tsp.gov

A repayment schedule is set up through payroll deduction, so provided you stay employed for the entirety of the repayment, there are no checks to write and no need to remember to pay the bill. If you leave federal service you must pay the loan back within 90 days. The time period over which the loan will be paid back is from one to five years for a general purpose loan, which can be for any purpose and requires no financial documentation, and between one and fifteen years if the loan is for the purpose of the purchase or construction of a primary residence. This latter option requires documentation as such. The interest you will pay is based on the G Fund rate at the time the loan is processed. This means in today's low interest rate environment a U.S. Treasury bond, generally one of the lowest yielding vehicles, is determining the cost of borrowing, and once in place this rate is fixed for the life of the loan, even if rates rise in the future. Not a bad deal.

It's often said, as I did earlier in this section, that an additional advantage of taking a loan is that the interest you are paying is credited to your balance as you pay it, so it could be construed as a method of increasing your overall savings. While this is possible, it's not always the case, because you have to consider the fact that you are also losing the investment performance of the balance that otherwise would be in the plan. So if you take a loan of $10,000 and the interest is 3% per year or $300, yes, that money will end up in your TSP balance when it otherwise would not have. Alternatively, if the $10,000 was just left in the plan and earned 5% or $500, then from a pure return standpoint you would be better off not taking the loan, not accounting for whatever you did with the $10,000 in this scenario. Talk to a financial advisor prior to electing the loan as the best option, and pat yourself on the back for choosing a plan that has this option.

What to Do for the Rest of Us

It is possible to successfully retire even if you don't have the comprehensive flexibility the TSP plan offers. It's the equivalent of using a car to get where you're going. If your goal is to get down the street and the car has an engine and four wheels on it, and you recognize that if your goal is the destination, not how you look while getting there, you will arrive. The key is to save. There are many standardized answers to how much is necessary, most of which cause more trepidation than inspiration.

The important thing, again, is to save. Create a budget and set money aside in as many different ways as you can, meaning both pre-tax and after-tax. If you don't have a tolerance for risk, then use safe vehicles like a CD or fixed annuity. If you use these safe vehicles, work with the plan guidelines you have to create a portfolio that's built for the long term. Review these choices with a financial advisor to ensure you're on the right track and doing everything you can.

Contact HR at your company to walk through each of these features to see which ones your plan offers and which ones it doesn't. This may be one of the main advantages you have in the private sector. Many work for small employers where the individuals responsible for the plan are close friends and colleagues who have authority over some of the options. You might find the plan does really offer target date funds but they were recently added, or perhaps the contact there has not heard of the Roth option but has the authority to add it simply by processing some paperwork, allowing you to generate tax-free income in retirement.

4
CHAPTER

Long-Term Care

Long term care is a serious issue. Hundreds of thousands of dollars can be spent on care and people are living much longer than prior generations. Health related costs are one of the most concerning topics retirees face as they plan the rest of their life. Whether you are private sector or federal there are options available to you that we will discuss here. We will first look at an example of how it can affect a family.

Sally was a widow by the age of 65. "It was really sad, of course, for a while, but eventually you just pick up the pieces and move on," she said.

She and John had a great life together. They were married for 38 years before he died. They had three wonderful children together and successfully retired by the time she was 60.

This chapter discusses a topic that is drastically changing our country's future. Mankind as a whole has never been through an aging process like this in its history. It will take courage on the part of our leaders, difficult discussions among families, and a lot of money to manage what's coming. Here, we walk through some planning options available to federal employees, and those offered by the private marketplace.

Sally recalls, "So we had five years in retirement together, and we traveled all over the world for his job over the last decade before that. Now I live for the grandbabies! I have six total and one on the way. John took care of the finances, and learning that part after he passed away was the hardest part. But we paid the house off, and I receive a small pension along with Social Security so I don't really worry about money. We built up $700,000 between John's life insurance and IRAs and I only take out about 2% of that a year. The rest I like to be conservative about, despite the rates, because I just don't want to lose. I don't really spend a lot, but I'm comfortable. The house, even after the downturn, is worth about $300,000, so on paper I'm a millionaire! Who would have thought?"

"I'm the poorest millionaire you'll ever meet," she'd say to her children, meaning she lived just fine off the $4,000 combined monthly income from all sources. She said, "I really want this money to go to the kids. They all work hard and have kids themselves to put through college and maybe graduate school. Those younger ones will need all the education they can get to make it in life these days."

When John and Sally were in their mid-fifties they considered the option of long-term care insurance. It seemed very expensive, and who knew whether they would need it or not? "I'll take care of you if something happens, Sally," John had said, "and I'm indestructible!" So they passed on the coverage and kept their money invested for the future. It wasn't $700,000 then because some of that was life insurance when John passed away, but it was a lot to them and they didn't want to incur expenses unnecessarily.

One day Sally's daughter started to notice that Sally was becoming more forgetful. "She'd lose track of things and forget things she had known like the back of her hand. I'd tell her she was trying to do too much at once, but it started to feel like something was wrong," her daughter said.

Sally was diagnosed with Alzheimer's along with arthritis in her joints. Modern medicine allowed the doctors to do amazing things, and Sally went on for years before the Alzheimer's really started to take over.

At first, just a little bit more was taken out of the assets to cover the prescriptions and someone coming by the house to check on her. She didn't want to leave the house, so they paid to have care brought in. Eventually, the comprehensive care offered by a local facility proved to be necessary, and Sally moved there. This care eventually started to force the children to spend about $5,000 a month of their mother's assets beyond the pensions.

"At this rate, the whole $700,000 could be gone," they said. They had sold the house, which helped, but the idea of using so much of the assets that she and John had worked so hard to save seemed heartbreaking.

"We love that she will be with us for as long as possible, especially the good days," her daughter said, "and we would never dream of anything but the best for Mom, but the family could really use that money one day. Who knows how long this will continue?"

This is an example of what can happen today in the world of planning around long-term care when people are living a lot longer than they used to. I don't mean to use these two people as a typical case, or to document stubbornness in some clients, because the perspective of "who knows what will happen" is a true liability to good planning. Who knows what will happen, indeed? It could be that the premium for long-term care insurance on two individuals, if saved instead, could accumulate to a sizable enough sum after taxes along the way to pay for an entire grandchild's college education, and it could be that neither of the two people will ever need anything more than a cane with which to walk. Statistically, though, it's likely at least one of the two of a household will need care beyond what normal health insurance will cover. And just like all insurance, it is much more efficient to transfer the risk of this occurrence to the insurance company than to assume everything will be all right.

According to a report by AARP published in the NAIC's *A Shopper's Guide to Long-Term Care*, "The lifetime probability of becoming disabled in at least two activities of daily living or being cognitively impaired is 68% for people age 65 and older." AARP is a well-known organization that provides many services to older Americans, and the NAIC is the National Association of Insurance Commissioners, which, among other things, tracks the long-term care insurance policies sold within members' respective states. Activities of daily living are dressing, eating, transferring (in and out of bed), grooming, ambulating (walking without assistance), and bladder management.

Before going into how exactly one "transfers" this risk successfully and for a reasonable cost, long-term care is a particular topic that warrants some explanation.

Medicare does not cover long-term care. Long-term care can be received in a number of different environments. A good explanation of the varying types is offered by the National Care Planning Council at the following website:

http://www.longtermcarelink.net/

Care can be given by a family member or a licensed caregiver at home. Alternatively, a facility can provide the care through either skilled nursing home care or what's called unskilled or custodial care. There's nothing "unskilled" about it, of course, because this occupation requires a unique blend of medical knowledge, patience, generosity to other human beings, and even physical strength. The uniqueness of these combined skills is so pronounced, in fact, that this occupation, along with that of nursing home facility workers, has the most worker shortages of any position in the country. Growth in the field is expected to be among the highest of any occupation over the entire next generation. There are also residences, called continuing care retirement communities (CCRCs) that offer the option of moving in, even with perfect physical and mental faculties. CCRCs are simply over-55 communities that make arrangements for any care that may be needed over time.

Regardless of these options, the nationwide program Medicare, even when combined with any of its alphabetic supplements, does not cover this type of care beyond a certain point. Generally, this amounts to approximately 100 days of health care at most and only after a hospital stay, but check with your current policy and supplements to find out the particulars in your own case. After 100 days or whatever the maximum is, the care will either be paid for by the person's assets, the insurance the person has purchased, or Medicaid.

Medicaid is a federal and state partnership program by which long-term care may be covered, provided that all financial resources have been exhausted by the individual. Although it is common practice to do everything possible, including seeking out legal counsel, to avoid having to sacrifice any assets and still qualify for Medicaid, or to never have to go anywhere near it, I would like to say that all of us should consider ourselves exceptionally fortunate to live in a country and at a time in human evolution where a government can implement a program that offers comprehensive medical care regardless of the financial toll any one individual causes the system. Millions of people every day are positively affected by the capabilities this program offers despite its imperfections. Politics and sustainability aside, this is a true blessing to many people.

As mentioned, though, Medicaid does require the person to have no remaining financial resources. I remember meeting with a client who had reached the age of 88 and whose assets consisted of Social Security and the clothes on her back. Her daughter, at her own expense, was trying to care for her at home with licensed caregivers stopping in, but it proved to be too difficult because her mother needed constant medical attention. The paperwork was filed to apply for Medicaid and eventually she was accepted at a facility. One other asset was uncovered, however. She had a $5,000 life insurance policy, purchased decades before, which required no further premiums and contained approximately $2,500 of cash value. The cash would never have been accessed otherwise, and the policy had an invaluable duty of providing liquid funds for funeral arrangements at the eventual end, which the daughter could sorely use. However, to be able to enter the facility, Medicaid processors required the policy to be cashed in and the proceeds be given over to the facility. At her inevitable passing about one year later, funeral arrangements were made but at the daughter's expense.

As the cost of this type of care can be enormous (see the following table), a consumer may choose the option of transferring the possible cost to an insurance company

The average costs for long-term care in the United States (in 2010) are:
$205 per day or $6,235 per month for a semi-private room in a nursing home
$229 per day or $6,965 per month for a private room in a nursing home
$3,293 per month for care in an assisted living facility (for a one-bedroom unit)
$21 per hour for a home health aide
$19 per hour for homemaker services
$67 per day for services in an adult day health care center

Source: http://www.longtermcare.gov

These are nationwide averages, and the local cost will vary widely depending on your state and the particular provider. Check out the long-term care website and click on your state for more specific information.

Once approved by an insurance company, and provided premiums are paid, a certain allotment of money is made available, generally on a daily or monthly basis, to reimburse the insured for paying the qualified bill. There are three items to be aware of here.

First, you must be approved by the insurance company. This involves a medical underwriting process consisting of questions, an attending physician statement, and in some cases blood and urine samples.

So, in the private marketplace it's not a given that thorough planning, taking the time to apply, and having the funds to insure this risk will even do the trick. One may be rated, causing the premium to be higher, or disqualified altogether based on previous medical circumstances. Not only does this burden the planning options of the household, but could signal concerns for their future health care needs. In other words, if the insured is declined, it statistically means he or she is more likely to need care.

Second, premiums must be paid on a continual basis. This means the insured must stay in a financial condition to be able to cover insurance premiums despite adjustments to those premiums. Most long-term care insurance policies are what are called guaranteed renewable. This term means, in general, that the insurance may not raise the rate on an individual policyholder. It may, however, raise rates on a class of policies, or all of its policies, even after they have been in force for a number of years, provided it meets the conditions for doing so.

This generally entails obtaining permission of the state insurance commissioner to raise rates and notifying all policy owners of the option to adjust their coverage in an effort to maintain the policy. This, unfortunately, has happened to enough policyholders, by enough insurance companies, to cause a proverbial black eye to the relatively young industry. Not necessarily to defend the insurance companies but to explain the process, the rates they charge are based on the statistical analysis of endless data on the unknowable possibility of what percentage of aging Americans will need care, what level and extent of care they will need, and what that care will cost, given our overall "managed care" society, now and decades into the future. This is not exactly an easy task.

Lastly, the insurance proceeds are "reimbursed" to the insured after paying a bill of a qualifying nature. This entails meeting the definition of care, which in general means not being able to perform at least two activities of daily living without substantial assistance or having a cognitive impairment or chronic illness that the medical community expects to last longer than 90 days.

It also entails, in most cases, producing a bill. Some plans do not require this reimbursement feature and instead allow the policy to pull benefits from the policy with more flexibility, even to compensate a spouse or family member for the care. This is referred to as an indemnity plan.

Although a family member may be the most readily available caregiver, and may do so at the most efficient cost, that person will not always qualify as the caregiver entitled to reimbursement. If you currently have or are shopping for long-term care insurance, be sure to ask what types of insurance benefits are available.

How does all this relate to federal government employees? In the private sector there are almost no employer-sponsored programs that allow employees to purchase long-term care insurance with any sort of volume pricing or payroll deduction capability. An article in *U.S. News and World Report*'s Money section on August 11, 2011, listed long-term care as one of the six retirement benefits in decline, despite the increased need for awareness and protection against this expensive exposure. The article is available at the following website:

http://money.usnews.com/money/blogs/
planning-to-retire/2011/08/03/6-retirement-benefits-in-decline

It states that a survey conducted recently showed only 29% of employers offered any such benefit. Incidentally, the article went on to state that pensions (Chapter 1 in this book), 401(k) matches (Chapter 2), retiree health insurance (Chapter 6), and phased retirement programs (Chapter 8) rounded out the benefits becoming extinct in the private sector.

There was discussion in 2010 of a possible national individually available long-term care plan through what's called the CLASS Act, or Community Living Assistance Services and Supports. It was part of the overall "Affordable Care Act" passed by the Obama administration and Congress. However, as of October 2011 it was announced that the long-term care portion of the Act would be unaffordable.

That gives you an idea of the size of the problem — when the entire federal government decides it can't afford it.

The Federal LTC Insurance Program (FLTCIP)

There is a program available only to employees of the federal government and their spouses, children, parents, and even retirees. It offers systemization of this process, free and organized resources for the purchaser.

Some of the features of the federal program are the following:

- Abbreviated underwriting (although rare)
- Competitive pricing for single insured
- Website and streamlined plan offering

Abbreviated Underwriting

Usually when applying for long-term care insurance there is a complete application asking several questions concerning one's medical history. There is then an interview with a nurse clarifying points on the application as well as other health questions, including some questions to determine if the early markers for dementia or Alzheimer's exist. Finally, a copy of the potential insured's medical records are ordered and all material submitted is analyzed by the underwriter. Using the information provided, an offer for coverage is made, or the person is declined.

If there is an offer it may be better, as expected, or more expensive than what the original quote outlined, because that is only an estimate. With this offer, the individual decides whether to take the coverage, take an adjusted version of the coverage, or not continue. This narrowing-down process is meant to reduce what's called adverse selection (the tendency for the unhealthiest applicants to go out and buy the coverage while the healthiest ones avoid it). In individual financial planning, adverse selection works in the opposite way. Discussing the options available to a couple who are likely to need long-term care due to their health have obviously fewer options because they can't transfer that risk away. With the federal program, there is a schedule to determine how much underwriting is required, and in the case of the eligible employee, it is easier to fulfill than the private marketplace. To be eligible one has to be newly hired, a spouse of the hired, or a recently married spouse of the employee.

Eligible Federal Employee – 2-, 3-, 5-Year Benefit	Seven questions about their health. No interview or health records.
Eligible Federal Employee – Unlimited Benefit	Several questions, possible interview and records.
Spouse of Eligible Employee – 2-, 3-, 5-Year Benefit	Nine questions about their health. No interview or health records.
Spouse of Eligible Employee – Unlimited Benefit	Several questions, possible interview and records.
Family of Employee and all others Eligible	Full Underwriting

The benefit period listed in the table explains how long benefits would be paid out provided the insured remains in need of and is receiving care. Insurance reimbursements generally happen on a daily or monthly basis, and as the table outlines, may continue for two years, three years, five years, or an unlimited number of years. Each successive increase in the benefit period corresponds to an increase in the required premium. Obtaining this type of insurance is an important decision that should be discussed with family members because there may be unique circumstances, such as the availability of a child to perform certain health care functions, or alternatively a single individual who needs access to care for as long as possible. According to the following website, the average stay for a resident, not a patient for temporary rehabilitation, in a nursing facility is 2.44 years (does not include staying in facilities such as assisted living or receiving care at home):

> http://www.longtermcarelink.net

Competitive Pricing for Single Insured

Both couples and individuals can apply for long-term care insurance. This is true of both the private marketplace and the federal program. Many times in the private marketplace when a couple applies together there is a discount given to both policies to reflect the fact that statistically speaking there's more of a chance of one spouse taking care of the other prior to reporting a claim. Said differently, individuals applying for coverage will pay more for an identical policy regardless of their health profile because this discount won't be applied. In the federal program there is no distinction between a couple and individuals when applying for coverage. Therefore, an unmarried individual may have the opportunity to save premiums by obtaining it through the federal program. Doing this doesn't ensure it's the best option, however, because in the private marketplace there are a wide variety of options that allow the purchaser to more thoroughly customize the policy, and more than just cost should be considered.

Website and Streamlined Plan Offering

The following website is a resource entirely devoted to the federal long-term care offering:

> http://www.ltcfeds.com/

It offers resources on planning for long-term care and the ability to directly apply and review billing and policy details through a sign-in feature. Applying for coverage is structured through this Web-based, streamlined prepackaged benefits system. You may also customize the benefit amount and period, but the prepackaged plans are made readily available. They offer either a $150 or $200 daily benefit, and either a 2-year, 3-year, or 5-year benefit. All options come with a 90-day waiting period. This is the duration of time before which benefits will be payable. This works similarly to a deductible, where a small initial period is the responsibility of the insured, only here it is expressed as a measure of time rather than a dollar amount. It is a dollar amount, of course, because care needs to be delivered for a cost during the 90 days and is paid out of pocket. In some cases, health insurance or a Medicare supplement will cover the costs of these 90 days.

Disadvantages

The federal program is not perfect. There are also the following disadvantages to be aware of:

- The program used to be a joint offering.
- There has been a 25% rate increase.
- No discount for excellent health/applying as spouses.
- It doesn't qualify under the state partnership plans.

Used to Be a Joint Offering

When the program originally became available it was jointly underwritten by two large stable insurance companies, Met Life and John Hancock, which formed the partnership company Long Term Care Partners, LLC. So, applicants had the peace of mind of not only having a quality policy but one that was backed by more than one insurance company. However, in 2009 as adjustments were made to the plan, John Hancock became the overall underwriter of the offering. John Hancock is still a highly-rated carrier and one the largest providers of long-term care insurance in the private market.

25% Rate Increase

In 2009 the announcement was made that premiums for existing policyholders would be raised, in some cases as much as 25%. This reflects the universal experience of insurers in the marketplace today that pricing coverage for an enormous number of aging insureds while simultaneously assessing the future cost of providing that care is proving difficult. Existing policyholders with the federal program, as with private insurers raising rates, were given the option of reducing benefits to maintain the same premium rather than accepting the higher cost.

No Health or Spousal Discounts

With privately purchased long term care there is an underwriting process just like the federal plan. The difference is if you are in excellent health you may receive a discount on the annual premium. Additionally some plans offer an additional discount if two spouses apply and purchase coverage at the same time. All who are considering this insurance coverage should determine if these opportunities exist in their comparison shopping.

State Partnership Plans

Because long term care services are expansive some individuals either don't have the assets to pay for the care, or run out of assets prior to passing away. In both cases depending on the financial circumstances Medicaid may step in and pay the cost of the care. Medicaid is administered primarily at the state level. To deal with these costs the states have created what are referred to as "State Partnership Plans". These are specifically designed, and privately purchased, long term care insurance policies that provide an added benefit beyond the coverage. Check with the state and the insurance company for specific details however in general it works as follows. If someone purchases a qualified policy with a total of $150,000 benefits, files a claim for LTC services, and eventually exhausts the policy Medicaid will allow the individual to keep $150,000 in their estate to pass on to beneficiaries, and still qualify for Medicaid services.

What to Do for the Rest of Us

Long-term care in America is a big issue. There are millions of people who will need care over the coming decades, and providing it may cost hundreds of thousands of dollars per person. Provided you are not eligible for the federal plan discussed in this chapter, there are still several things you can do. They are listed individually so that they may be considered one by one, although in many cases they are used in combination.

- Let family take care of you.
- Buy private long-term care insurance.
- Buy combination Life/Long-term care insurance.
- Set assets aside.

Let Family Take Care of You

This isn't so much a plan as a lack of one. Although it has changed in the last few generations, this was pretty much the standard response to aging family members. These days, however, you have more complex diagnoses, more advanced treatments, busier and far-flung family, longer periods of care, and, frankly, larger patients. With only Mom and Dad left at home and weighing in at 140 lbs. and 220 lbs., respectively, it's not too likely Mom can handle too many physically debilitating illnesses with Dad. If you choose this option, though, the best advice I can provide is to have some thorough discussions with family so everyone is on the same page if a health event occurs. Also put the result of these discussions in writing through the use of legal documents. These take the form of a health care power of attorney, medical directive, or do not resuscitate order, among others. These documents should be created regardless of whether someone purchases long-term care insurance, but they are especially necessary if you have no other arrangements in place.

Buy Private Long-Term Care Insurance

Long-term care insurance is essentially buying a pile of money that's made available in certain circumstances. The insurance company makes these funds available to you and your family should there be a health event that requires qualified medical care beyond what normal health insurance and its supplements cover. The value is obviously that the pile of money wasn't yours prior to purchasing the policy, but now, if care is needed, you can use their money instead of your own.

If you don't end up needing care, your beneficiaries don't get to keep the insurance company's money, but in exchange you lived the later years of your life without requiring substantial assistance to get by, or at least you didn't need to pay for this assistance. This is peace of mind. People should value this transfer of risk, but some don't. It's understandable because the coverage can be expensive. A couple age 65 in average health can expect to pay several thousand dollars per year for policies insuring each of them. The key here is to buy something. Estates can be erased due to this newfound societal problem, so a full policy offering several thousand dollar a month of benefit is always preferred, and a good financial planner should show you how to find the best offering and walk through a budget process to show you how to afford it.

But even if the underwriting doesn't go so well, or the benefit isn't as high as the cost in your area, buy something. Put the insurance company on the hook for some of the cost of this care. You will spend the rest of your retirement at least having some peace of mind and just as important you'll also be able to communicate with the company about care options. No one I've worked with over the years has grown old and decided they regretted owning a policy. And many ended up needing much more of the policy than they realized.

You should look for a few particular features in your long-term care policy. This is by no means an exhaustive list, just the initial terms you will need to understand. These are:

1. Daily vs. monthly benefit
2. Compound vs. simple inflation
3. Benefit period

The first is the daily or monthly benefit. This is the dollar amount the insured can use on a daily or monthly basis to cover the costs of the care. Ideally, you want a monthly benefit. It's easier for claims reporting purposes, and if the insureds are receiving care on an intermittent basis, meaning not necessarily daily, they can aggregate the bills over a month and receive reimbursement more efficiently.

Second, the cost of a month's worth of care in any given area can vary widely, but if you have $6,000 or more benefit in today's dollars, that will cover most claims. The cost of care is going up so you may want to factor this in to your monthly benefit amount. You can either accomplish this through a higher monthly benefit from the beginning of the policy or by purchasing inflation protection. This causes the benefit to increase on an annual basis at a compound or simple rate (say, 5% of the original amount). This is usually one of the first benefits to get reduced when prospective buyers are looking at saving some money. It's also usually the first benefit to get reduced when existing policies get a rate increase.

As explained earlier, insurance companies can raise rates on classes of policies if claims end up being worse than expected. What will happen when they announce this adjustment, however, is to offer options. The policyholder can either accept the rate increase, or accept an alternative such as keeping the premium the same in exchange for a removal or reduction of the inflation protection on the monthly benefit.

This is a difficult decision, so if you have existing insurance, don't rush to a conclusion or use the letter as a reason to cancel the coverage entirely. Maintain as high a monthly benefit as possible; because this provides the most flexibility should a claim occur.

Third, on long-term care insurance policies there will be a benefit period. This is the number of months the policy will pay that claim to reimburse the insured for the cost of care. It is generally between two and five years, but there are policies that offer an unlimited claim period. These policies are less prevalent in today's marketplace because they represent an unlimited risk to the company. If cost is prohibiting you from purchasing a full 4- to 5-year policy and you are choosing between reducing the benefit period and reducing the monthly benefit, all other things being equal, the shorter benefit period will provide more flexibility. The reason is that if the monthly benefit is $8,000 and the period is three years, you can spend the full $8,000 or leave some in for later, as long as the cost is $8,000 or higher. If the cost is $8,000, on the other hand, and the monthly benefit is $6,000 with a 4-year benefit, you're going to be out of pocket $2,000 every month, even if the policy is providing full benefits.

Buy Combination Life/Long-Term Care (LTC)

Due to the drawbacks of traditional long-term care insurance, there is a lot of interest today surrounding combination or hybrid polices. These are not your parents' long-term care policies! They combine a long-term care policy within another benefit like a savings vehicle or a life insurance policy. In some cases, this type of coverage makes even more sense than buying regular long-term care. One example of this coverage is a life insurance policy, meaning it pays a tax-free death benefit if the insured passes away. However, if the insured becomes sick and needs funds for care in a facility or at home, the insured can pull funds out of the death benefit, tax-free, to cover these expenses. How would you like to combine these coverages into one easy-to-manage policy and know that if you live a good long life and never need care, the premiums you have been paying all those years won't go to waste? The beneficiary(ies) you name will inherit tax-free cash that can be used to pay off the remainder of the mortgage or other debts, or be used to replace lost income due to your death.

Now there's a cost for this policy. It is underwritten as a life insurance policy, and the company will also ask questions of the insured about health-related circumstances that could lead to a LTC claim in the future. As long as you're approved for this type of policy, it is a strong option that protects against multiple risks you may face as a household. An alternative form of a combination policy involves an asset-driven instrument where funds are deposited into an account and it, in general, buys a multiple of that deposit for long-term care costs. What's convenient about these policies is that the deposit, subject to some restrictions, can be accessed back if needed by the policyholder for purposes other than long-term care.

The policyholder may also buy a multiple of the deposit in the form of life insurance as well, thereby creating a three-in-one benefit: life insurance, long-term care insurance, and interest on your money. Another asset-driven strategy involves using an annuity. Some annuity contracts today will offer a stream of income that adjusts upward if there is a nursing home stay or an inability to perform the necessary activities of daily living. All these alternatives to normal LTC insurance come with advantages and disadvantages. Research your options, work with a good planner, and express your wishes. Your family will thank you if something happens.

Set Assets Aside

If the underwriting process for one of the policies above doesn't go favorably, or you make a family decision to not transfer this risk to an insurance company, you are making a default decision to either do nothing or to identify certain assets that will cover the care should you need it. Doing this has the obvious advantages of getting to avoid paying a bill every year and retaining control of the asset you have identified. The downside is that you never know whether that asset will be sufficient to cover the cost of care; there may not be an asset large enough to set aside without needing it for living expenses, and taxes will generally need to be paid on these funds as they pay interest or dividends or as distributions occur.

On IRA funds there won't be income tax due until distributions begin from the asset. Ideally, these distributions will only occur when care is needed if it truly is set aside for this purpose. On IRA funds, though, taxable withdrawals need to start at age 70.5 through what's called required minimum distributions (RMD). This limits the asset's ability to be preserved for later use on care costs as they grow over time.

Although these distributions are considered income and taxable as such, if the funds coming out are indeed being used for medical expenses over a long term, there can be some deductions.

A continuing care retirement community (CCRC) is a retirement community that can expand or contract the level of care it provides based on the ups and downs of growing old. CCRCs are one of the latest advances in dealing with our aging society. Couples or elderly individuals will move into these facilities, in many cases in fine health but with the goal of having the convenience of ongoing care should it become necessary. These facilities are great options for retired individuals, and I will work with many clients to discuss the financial aspects of transitioning to this type of environment. Most places will require a sizable entry fee and then a monthly fee based on the size of the home you choose and/or the amenities to which you will be entitled. The entry fee will generally be in the hundreds of thousands of dollars. Usually people are selling their primary residence to come up with this fee. The house is now too big to take care of, the kids are gone, the maintenance is more of a nuisance than part of the pride of homeownership, and now a simpler life is available in this new type of living. Sometimes the couple will resist this strategy, thinking the residence has grown into a family heirloom that should be passed down to the children as an inheritance. However, I often find that the children, especially in this real estate market, would rather not inherit the property and want the best, most comprehensive care for their parents.

The kids may have a house of their own to deal with, or may be unable to come to an understanding between themselves on the disposition plan. It would be a more complex decision for the retiree if the sale of the house was an irrevocable arrangement for the entry fee, meaning kept at death by the CCRC. Fortunately, it is not. In most cases, upon death this deposit is returned to beneficiaries to the extent it was not tapped during the resident's stay.

Beyond this entry fee, there is a monthly amount due as rent. This will vary depending on the size of the home. It can be a few thousand dollars a month and increase further if a couple is moving in as opposed to one individual doing so, so it is not cheap. However, these monthly fees are designed to cover a variety of possible living situations, including skilled nursing care when necessary. What's even better is if financial resources dwindle and the residents can no longer fully cover the monthly fee, the facility will begin to utilize the initial deposit as payment. And if the initial deposit were to be completely depleted, the tenant is guaranteed a continuation of care and residence for the remainder of his or her life. If you're considering this option, look into it thoroughly. Have a family discussion about the property and visit multiple locations in your area to compare features. Also see a tax advisor and a financial planner on the tax consequences of selling your residence and setting up an income stream to cover the monthly fee.

CHAPTER 5

Social Security

Social Security is available to all workers who pay FICA taxes, which represents 96% of the population in America today. Due to the changes in the pension system in 1984, federal employees hired after that point in time are included in this category. Let's look at Bill and Kelly.

Bill and Kelly both worked and earned good incomes. Bill was a manager for the government, and Kelly worked for a consulting firm. Bill was FERS, meaning he got a pension when he retired, but they just assumed they had to keep working because the calculation of what the pension would be always showed a number so much smaller than what they were making combined. They saved when they could, but due to market performance they only had in their accounts what they had contributed over time. They had both worked consistently, though, so their earnings records were good. They both made over six figures for the last several years at their respective jobs.

This chapter outlines Social Security, which is a benefit available to all individuals except CSRS employees. Therefore, we will outline its features and advantages as well as point out some methods by which retirees can maximize their benefits.

"How do we go from $230k down to $40,000 like my pension estimate says?" Bill asked. They consistently paid in to Social Security but had never really paid attention to the estimates. "We won't get that. They'll reduce that or keeping moving the carrot out so we have to be like 75 before we can collect," Bill said.

Well, that may be for some, but Bill and Kelly actually made it to full retirement age, and we ran the numbers again. Because of their consistent work records — Bill had worked for the government since 1987, and Linda had a few jobs but never went too long without landing a new one — they were pleasantly surprised by the numbers. They both would begin collecting Social Security at full retirement age, 66 for both of them, and are entitled to $2,200 and $1,800 a month, respectively.

"That's $48,000 a year!" Bill said. It was before health care premiums and taxes, but yes, it was $48,000 a year. Bill added, "Between that and my pension, we will have about $90,000 a year coming in. We could sell the place and move to the beach like we talked about and live very well on that. And that's without even touching our assets."

Social Security is a politically divisive issue. In the early 1930s when it was created, the goal was to create jobs. Older workers had no support system to allow retirement, and those who hadn't saved enough money, which was even more difficult than than it is today, had to keep working. If they could be given a basic subsistence of income, their employers could bring on younger workers to replace them. The disagreement these days, though, is mostly about adjustments needed to the program to ensure its viability, not the merits of whether it should exist at all. The millions of people who subsist on those monthly checks can attest to the lifesaving features Social Security provides compared to what less fortunate economies can afford. We really do live in a magnificent country with countless opportunities to lead a rewarding, long life full of contributions to society, to make a difference, and to raise a family. Every once in a while there is the opinion offered that if people could opt out of Social Security and invest or allocate those taxes elsewhere they could come out ahead. For the masses of people, though, Social Security represents a vital, reliable source of retirement income despite its imperfections.

According to Social Security's 2011 trustee report, retirement income checks alone totaled $606 billion for that calendar year. Think about that for a moment. That means the federal government pays out $1.6 billion every single day in checks to its retired citizens to spend any way they see fit. These citizens stop working and collect Social Security benefits as one of the sources of income they use to enjoy the later years of their life, which in some cases may last decades. The government guarantees these checks will come in regardless of how long the retiree lives. It also offers the opportunity for those checks to increase annually due to inflation (CPI/W) and makes certain provisions for survivorship income, depending on the circumstances.

You have to pay taxes over time when you're working to get Social Security, and you may have to pay taxes on the money when it comes out, depending on your total income (see later in this chapter for details). The system is paying out more than it collects at the moment. There are other problems with Social Security, but it's still a great entitlement that citizens of this country should be, and for the most part are, thankful for. I don't have too many clients walk into my office and say they are leaving the country because they don't think this Social Security thing is a good enough deal. Now because Social Security is there and this is a free country where people are motivated to earn every advantage they can in life, there's no harm in understanding the system and using it to its full advantage. That's where a good financial planner comes in who knows the rules and can guide a family through their working years into their beneficiary years as productively as possible. Let's take a look at some of the features Social Security offers:

- Retirement income
- Favorable tax arrangement
- Disability income

Retirement Income

Just like Bill and Kelly, you may be entitled to a Social Security check every month starting as early as age 62. Your full retirement age is different, however, and there is a reduction for starting your payment early. The following table lets you determine your full retirement age (FRA).

1. If you were born on January 1st, you should refer to the previous year.
2. If you were born on the 1st of the month, we figure the benefit as if your birthday were in the previous month. You must be at least 62 for the entire month to receive benefits.
3. Percentages are approximate due to rounding.
4. The maximum benefit for the spouse is 50% of the benefit the worker would receive at full retirement age. The % reduction for the spouse should be applied after the automatic 50% reduction. Percentages are approximate due to rounding.

Social Security

Year of Birth [1]	Full (normal) Retirement Age	Months between age 62 and full retirement age	At Age 62 [2]				The spouse's benefit is reduced by [4]
			A $1,000 retirement benefit would be reduced to	The retirement benefit is reduced by [3]	A $500 spouse's benefit would be reduced to		
1937 or earlier	65	36	$800	20%	$375	25%
1938	65 & 2 months	38	$791	20.83%	$370	25.83%
1939	65 & 4 months	40	$783	21.67%	$366	27.50%
1940	65 & 6 months	42	$775	22.5%	$362	26.67%
1941	65 & 8 months	44	$766	23.33%	$358	28.33%
1942	65 & 10 months	46	$758	24.17%	$354	29.17%

Total Compensation: A Practical Guide to Federal Employee Benefits

1943-1954	66	48	$750	25.0%	$350	30.0%
1955	66 & 2 months	50	$741	25.83%	$345	30.83%
1956	66 & 4 months	52	$733	26.67%	$341	31.67%
1957	66 & 6 months	54	$725	27.50%	$337	32.50%
1958	66 & 8 months	56	$716	28.33%	$333	33.33%
1959	66 & 10 months	58	$708	29.17%	$329	34.17%
1960 & later	67	60	$700	30.0%	$325	35.0%

Source: http://www.ssa.gov/retire2/agereduction.htm#chart

This table displays several things. It shows, depending on the year of your birth, how old you have to be to reach full retirement age. There is not one retirement age for everyone — the table shows a schedule for various ages. It also shows, in the fourth column difference between receiving $1,000 of income beginning at full retirement age and starting early. The column shows the amount you would receive if you started receiving benefits early. This lost income can add up. If you were born after 1960 but start taking payments at age 62, you will receive $300 less a month for life. And cost of living adjustments, when they occur, will always be a percentage of this lower figure.

The last column here is important because it shows something that not everyone is aware of about Social Security. Spouses will receive a benefit that is equal to their own earnings record over the years, or if they didn't work or didn't work very much, they will receive a benefit based on their spouse's earnings. Many couples are not aware they are entitled to this benefit, but it means several hundred more dollars a month to them. The calculation for this income is the individual's own amount or half their spouse's, whichever is higher. That is why the above table shows $500 as a monthly benefit.

As the chart also indicates, though, this amount is reduced for beginning the payments early. A couple born after 1960 would receive 35% of the spouse's payment, or $325 a month. So for the couple in this example that is deciding when to take payments, they are looking at a difference between $1,500 ($1,000 + $500) and $1,025 ($700 + $325) a month. Not receiving $475 every month is forgoing a lot of money when you're looking at Social Security as your primary source of income. According to the following Social Security website, the average payment to a retiree as of June 2011 was $1,181 each month:

http://www.socialsecurity.gov/OACT/FACTS/

Favorable Tax Arrangement

Social Security is taxable, but not entirely. You have to look at the total picture of your income for the year, and in a worst-case scenario Social Security will still be one of the more tax-efficient sources. This is because rather than calling all income from it taxable, only a certain percentage is, based on the total income, including income from other sources. The IRS provides the following breakdown:

No one pays federal income tax on more than 85 percent of his or her Social Security benefits based on Internal Revenue Service (IRS) rules. If you:

- **File a federal tax return as an "individual"** and your combined income*is
    - Between $25,000 and $34,000, you may have to pay income tax on up to 50 percent of your benefits.
    - More than $34,000, up to 85 percent of your benefits may be taxable.
- **File a joint return**, and you and your spouse have a combined income* that is
    - Between $32,000 and $44,000, you may have to pay income tax on up to 50 percent of your benefits
    - More than $44,000, up to 85 percent of your benefits may be taxable.
- **Are married and file a separate tax return,** you probably will pay taxes on your benefits

*Note:	Your adjusted gross income + Nontaxable interest + ½ of your Social Security benefits = Your "**combined income**"

Source: http://www.ssa.gov/planners/taxes.htm

When the breakdown says "income" it means the total value of Social Security the household received will be added up with other sources like pensions and earned income. The totals are compared to these ranges above to determine how much is included for reporting on the tax return. Then the normal graduated scale is used to apply the tax. In the highest income range here, 85% of Social Security is included; meaning in no instance is all of your Social Security income reported.

Additionally, depending on your state of residence, income from Social Security may be exempt from tax at the state level as well. Few other types of retirement income offer this tax efficiency. Kiplinger's offers a convenient map tool to look up your state to consider the tax environment of the state you live in or may move to in retirement. It's available at the following website:

http://www.kiplinger.com/tools/retiree_map/

Let's look at a basic example of how income tax in retirement may be less costly than one might imagine. Keep in mind that this is a generalization based on 2011 tax schedules. See a tax advisor to have it applied to your situation and for specific tax advice.

Bill's Pension	$30,000
Bill's IRA withdrawals	$20,000
Bill's Social Security	$21,600
Kelly's Social Security	$18,000
Municipal Bond Interest	$10,400
Total	$100,000 Annual Income

Since Bill and Kelly file jointly, they are over Social Security's income limit with the pension and IRA withdrawals alone. This means 85% of their Social Security will be reported on their return as taxable income. So 85% of $39,600 is $33,660 plus the $50,000 of fully taxable income. The municipal bond interest, provided they are bonds issued in their state of residence, are exempt from federal and state income tax. So the total income here that would be applied to the graduated federal tax schedule is $83,660.

Presuming they take a standard deduction rather than itemize, perhaps because they paid the house down, they would deduct $11,600 from the total to bring it down to $72,260.

They also each receive a personal exemption of $3,700 to reduce the total to $64,860.

Then the schedule below applies.

Tax Bracket	Married Filing Jointly	Single
10% Bracket	$0 – $17,000	$0 – $8,500
15% Bracket	$17,001 – $69,000	$8,501 – $34,500
25% Bracket	$69,001 – $139,350	$34,501 – $83,600
28% Bracket	$139,351 – $212,300	$83,601 – $174,400
33% Bracket	$212,301 – $379,150	$174,401 – $379,150
35% Bracket	Over $379,150	Over $379,150

The first $17,000 will be in the 10% bracket, resulting in $1,700 of tax. The remaining $47,860 is in the 15% tax bracket which equals $7,179. Add to that $1,700, and you get $8,879. The original total income for Bill and Kelly was $100,000 and the tax was around $8,900 or an 8.9% effective rate. Thanks to diversifying their sources of income, and a little tax planning an 8.9% tax rate on a six-figure retirement income isn't bad!

Another way of maximizing a household's Social Security income is to use a tactic called claim and suspend. As explained earlier, spouses who didn't work as much as their partners are entitled to receive their own benefit or as much as 50% of their spouse's benefit, whichever is higher. This is a great feature of Social Security, but it is capped at 50%. No matter how long the higher earners work, their spouse's benefit will not grow to more than 50% of the amount the higher earner accrued. And lower-earning spouses cannot claim benefits off their spouse's record until that person files for benefits.

Let's say you have a 64-year-old stay-at-home mom and a 66-year-old husband who is still working and enjoys it. He's accruing benefits toward Social Security and doesn't want to stop working. However, the only way for his wife to begin receiving a payment is for him to file for Social Security. In this scenario, he can "claim and suspend," which allows his wife to claim and collect her benefit. This may result in several hundred or even over a thousand dollars extra a month coming in at a time when the couple could be making that final push toward retirement savings. By "suspending" his benefit, he will not receive any payments, but due to his employment income, payments are not needed. His benefit will keep accruing to age 70 or when he retires, whichever comes first.

Why is this planning option even more valuable? As also mentioned earlier, if one member of the household passes away, the survivor is entitled to the higher of the two benefits but not both. So in this scenario if the husband passed away prior to receiving any benefit, the stay-at-home mom never would have received any of her benefit anyway. She would file and receive 100% of his benefit as a survivor, but her entitlement would go away.

Federal workers will receive benefit summaries from Social Security annually that reflect their work record and an estimate of what they will receive in benefits. As some types of federal employees know well, however, this amount does not always take into account all the available data. If workers are employed under the Civil Service Retirement System (CSRS), even if they later were employed in a position where they paid Social Security taxes, they could be subject to the Windfall Elimination Provision (WEP), or the Government Pension Offset (GPO). Social Security describes the Windfall Elimination Provision like this:

The Windfall Elimination Provision primarily affects you if you earned a pension in any job where you did not pay Social Security taxes (like CSRS) and you also worked in the private sector long enough to qualify for a Social Security retirement or disability benefit.

For example, this provision affects Social Security benefits when any part of a person's federal service after 1956 is covered under the CSRS. However, federal service where Social Security taxes are withheld (FERS) will not reduce your Social Security benefit amounts. The Windfall Elimination Provision may apply if:

- You reached 62 after 1985; or
- You became disabled after 1985; and
- You first became eligible for a monthly pension based on work where you did not pay Social Security taxes after 1985, even if you are still working.

Source: http://ssa.gov/pubs/10045.html

In other words, if you work for the federal government under CSRS and then you go to work in the private sector in a job where you pay FICA taxes, any amount of Social Security this qualifies you for hypothetically will be adjusted downward in light of the government pension. Many times clients will receive the annual benefit statement from Social Security showing an amount as though they don't have their pension, causing a false sense of future additional income.

Similarly, the Government Pension Offset (GPO) refers to a reduction in Social Security the individual would receive as a dependent or survivor of someone who was receiving Social Security retirement benefits. If Bob was covered by CSRS and is now receiving a pension upon retirement, and his wife Lisa worked in the private sector and received Social Security, Bob would not be entitled to a spousal benefit, meaning the 50% amount described earlier, nor would he receive Lisa's Social Security if she predeceased him. A few assumptions are being made in this scenario, and how much of a reduction each person will or will not receive can be complicated. Review your specific situation with a financial planner and with your local Social Security office.

Disability Income

Income from Social Security doesn't always occur as a result of retirement. A disability can cause catastrophic financial consequences to a household.

The statistics are staggering. Over 5% of U.S. workers, 8.3 million disabled wage earners, were receiving Social Security Disability Insurance (SSDI) benefits at the conclusion of March 2011, according to the Social Security Administration. One in eight workers will be disabled for five years or more during their working careers, according to the federal government (see the following website):

http://www.disabilitycanhappen.org/chances_disability/disability_stats.asp

SSDI paid out $115,059,000,000 in benefits in 2010 alone. Once a disability occurs due to medical diagnosis or accident, most families are not financially equipped to handle it. A recent article in *The Journal of the American Medical Association* (JAMA) reported that medical problems contributed to 62% of all personal bankruptcies filed in the U.S. in 2007.

When a disability occurs, the first step is to take inventory of what assets you have. How much in liquid reserve funds do you have available? Do you have six months or more worth of living expenses? Do you know what your monthly expenses total? Do you know what your health insurance will cover and what it won't? An excellent resource if you find yourself in this situation is available at the following website:

http://www.disabilitycanhappen.org/

If it looks like recovery will take several months or years, the next step should be to apply for SSDI. Even if the disability is not expected to last for over a year, apply anyway. The process to qualify for benefits can take months alone, and setbacks in recovery can happen at a moment's notice.

When filing for disability benefits be sure to tell the local office, and your financial planner, whether you have dependents. A dependent child may be entitled to separate monthly income due to your disability. If the child is under age 18, or up to 19 while a full-time student, unmarried, and dependent on a disabled or deceased worker who has qualified for benefits, they are entitled to benefits. The child can receive 50% of the amount the disabled recipient is receiving, or 75% of what a deceased recipient's benefit amount was. There is a family cap that is applied that maxes out at 180% of the parent's full benefit amount and all amounts are reduced proportionately if the cap occurs. In an event like a disability or premature death, however, every source of income a family receives is vital.

Proposed Changes to Social Security

When explaining the benefits and best uses of Social Security to a client, I inevitably get the response, "Yeah, but they'll run out of money eventually, so I don't want to count that as one of my income sources." Given the lack of a clear plan from the people in Washington, this is an understandable concern. However, it's far more likely — for two reasons — that over time incremental changes will be made to the system to ensure its survival.

First, allowing it to collapse would cause unknowable harm to our economy and our country's support systems, not to mention infuriating a giant segment of reliable voters. Second, politicians know very well that once you give something valuable to your electorate it's almost impossible to take it away.

So what are the changes they are proposing? There are many of them, and probably more than one will be implemented as necessary, over the next several decades. Once this occurs, Social Security will be a less lucrative deal for retirees, but it will be a more reliable, flexible, and efficient version that people, specifically voters, will still value.

The following are some changes currently being discussed:

- Cost of living adjustments
- Level of monthly benefits
- Taxation
- Investment of trust fund assets in securities/individual Accounts
- Increase in payroll tax rate
- Increase of income limit for payroll tax
- Retirement age

Cost of Living Adjustments

Data gathered every year by the Bureau of Labor Statistics is analyzed to generate what is called the Consumer Price Index (CPI/W). Since consumers are the ones who survive on Social Security, the items they buy with it most correctly determines how it should increase from year to year.

A big caveat to this, of course, is that the relationship between each individual's cost increases and the enormous amount of data going into the CPI number are not always closely linked. For example the CPI/W, the measure of increase on Social Security, does not take into account health and energy costs.

A 72-year-old widow who doesn't drive very much and whose health insurance premiums, prescription drugs, property taxes, and long-term care insurance premiums went up by 10% doesn't really care if a nationwide calculation determined that the cost of gas, big-screen TVs, airline tickets, and baby food only went up by 2.3% last year. It's the system we have, though, and historically it has still provided the basis for meaningful increases in millions of people's main source of income.

The following table shows the data going back to 1975.

Social Security Cost-of-Living Adjustments						
Year	COLA		Year	COLA	Year	COLA
1975	8.0		1990	5.4	2005	4.1
1976	6.4		1991	3.7	2006	3.3
1977	5.9		1992	3.0	2007	2.3
1978	6.5		1993	2.6	2008	5.8
1979	9.9		1994	2.8	2009	0.0
1980	14.3		1995	2.6	2010	0.0
1981	11.2		1996	2.9	2011	3.6
1982	7.4		1997	2.1	2012	1.7
1983	3.5		1998	1.3		
1984	3.5		1999[a]	2.5		
1985	3.1		2000	3.5		
1986	1.3		2001	2.6		
1987	4.2		2002	1.4		
1988	4.0		2003	2.1		
1989	4.7		2004	2.7		

[a] The COLA for December 1999 was originally determined as 2.4 percent based on CPIs published by the Bureau of Labor Statistics. Pursuant to Public Law 106-554, however, this COLA is effectively now 2.5 percent.

One observation about this table is that the government has a strong vested interest in avoiding what happened from 1979 to 1982. Over that four-year time period the average Social Security recipient saw their payment increase by over 40%. This means that if recipients started out receiving $12,000 a year, they ended that four years receiving $16,800, and every annual increase they received after that was compounded on top of the new amount. Multiply that by the millions of people currently receiving benefits, and the 78,000,000 baby boomers knocking on the door.

Social Security

So the government has considered, and it's been discussed in various lobbying circles, restricting the possible increase each year to some maximum limit. Although this scenario is possible, it's more likely that other methods will be used to prevent such large increases. Medicare Part B premiums already come out of most people's Social Security checks, and the increases on these premiums usually absorb much or all of the CPI increase anyway. To limit the possible increase on Social Security while not handling the Medicare problem of rising costs would leave millions of recipients receiving less money year after year. Also, the CPI calculation may take care of limiting increases for years to come because borderline deflation grips our economy for the foreseeable future.

Level of Monthly Benefits

How much you receive in Social Security income is based on your lifetime earnings. Your earnings are "indexed" to account for changes in average wages since the year those earnings were received. Then Social Security calculates your average indexed earnings during the highest 35 years. They apply a formula to these earnings and arrive at your basic benefit or "primary insurance amount" (PIA). This rather lengthy calculation is carried out for each person over a 35-year time period at minimum.

It would be actuarially easy — although politically difficult — to adjust this formula so average benefits are lower, thereby saving the system millions of dollars a year when extended across all future recipients. While some adjustment to this formula is likely as the reality of the problem becomes more apparent, those who have worked and paid FICA taxes for years are unlikely in my opinion to see major changes. As bad as the numbers seem at the moment, small adjustments to any or a combination of Social Security's proposed changes can be phased in over a period of decades and cause major improvement to the overall financial picture. Younger workers, such as the ones not thinking about retirement being relatively close, and also probably not reading this book, could earn a few dollars less in retirement income from Social Security than what your FICA taxes earn you now.

Taxation

As explained earlier, there is a phase-in of taxability, topping at 85% of what a household receives going into the taxable income category for filing one's income tax return. This schedule, or the privilege of receiving at least some tax-free, may go away entirely. There are only two guarantees in life, right? Death and taxes. The key here is whether the politicians do the right thing relative to Social Security and tie this increase in taxes collected to putting the system itself on a solid footing financially, and not just institute a random increase to cover some other spending project. From a financial planning standpoint, the issue of taxes doesn't affect much of the strategy of planning for retirement. Not too many people would turn away the income simply because a portion of it is taxable when it previously wasn't.

Here's one approach to collecting Social Security if more of it becomes taxable, though. If you were delaying applying for benefits because of the tax efficiency and in its place withdrawals were being taken from taxable IRA accounts, the new tax requirement would make them equivalent. Therefore, it may make sense to begin taking payments from Social Security and giving the IRA investments a chance to grow (or at least recover). In other words, if they were taxed the same you might as well spend the government's money instead of your own. Again, that is only a strategy to consider if Congress changes the rules, so keep in touch with your tax professional on the status of these proposed tax changes. Another excellent way to stay on top of these provisions is through the following Social Security webpage, where you will find notices of proposals and their progress:

> http://www.ssa.gov/OACT/solvency/provisions/index.html

Investment of Trust Fund Assets in Securities/Individual Accounts

In the early part of the last decade the investment of Social Security Trust Fund assets in securities or individual accounts was an idea that got a lot of attention because of its consideration by the Bush Administration. These days, given the investment markets, this option is unlikely to be adopted anytime soon.

In the 1970s when ERISA, a comprehensive program concerning saving for retirement, was enacted and the 401(k) began its meteoric rise, the 401(k) essentially replaced pension plans over time. Investment of Social Security Trust Fund assets in securities or individual accounts would essentially be doing the same thing, supplanting the previous system. It's worth noting, though, that there is a huge difference between (1) allowing the Social Security Trust Fund to gradually diversify a small portion of its assets away from "special issue" government securities into highly rated corporate bonds or equities and (2) allowing all individuals complete investment discretion over the last backstop against poverty in their later years.

The Social Security Trust Fund is made up of billions of dollars (on paper at least), with a reliable supply of incoming tax dollars year after year. Some of the proposals for investing this money have taken into account the possibility that equity and bond returns could perform no better than the 2.9% (long-term average) for the special issue government bond used now. How much of the Trust Fund is allowed into investments will be difficult to determine. Right now some proposals call for a gradual increase to 15%, while others suggest 40%. For the recipients, little change should occur, because as the benefits would be guaranteed either way.

Individual accounts, on the other hand, would be a whole new game. Rather than having the formula for indexed earnings equating to a guaranteed amount of income, each person would have to navigate the investment markets, hope they cooperate, and then determine an appropriate distribution percentage and pass away prior to outliving their portfolio. This would be a difficult task even in good markets, so the volatility we are currently experiencing makes doing these things impractical. The idea of investing by individuals originated with the notion that the stock market had now officially reached Main Street anyway, so the majority of the country would be open to allocating assets to stocks and bonds.

We're not quite there yet, however. As recently as 2008, according to an ICI/SIFMA (The Investment Company Institute/the Securities Industry and Financial Markets Association) survey, about half of U.S. households had holdings in equities or bonds. This means millions of households have no positions at all in the markets. Whether this puts them at a disadvantage, or maybe an advantage, for their financial planning is the subject of another debate. But asking them to begin choosing investments to replace what was that last and possibly only reliable income source they had probably wouldn't work without major safeguards put in place.

It may be that some portion of these households aren't avoiding the markets because they do not have available assets to allocate but because they choose not to participate due to the uncertainty involved. If even 5% were unable to navigate the system properly, it would result in approximately 2,750,000 people without income who otherwise would have income. That's why, among the available options to the powers that be, individual accounts are probably going to be analyzed conservatively and vehemently opposed by many parties involved. If such accounts do receive eventual approval, they will need tremendous safeguards around them for the good of the average citizen.

Increase in Payroll Tax Rate

Increasing the payroll tax rate has already been tried—many times. So many times, in fact, that our forefathers would be ashamed. The following table from the Social Security website shows that the tax rate on earned income has been increased 19 times since its inception in 1937.

How much higher can it go? Currently, in 2011 and part of 2012, we have been given a reprieve in the form of a reduction on the employee side only from 6.2% back down to 4.2%, which is widely understood to be temporary.

In the table, OASDI stands for Old Age Survivors and Disability Insurance, which is the official name for the Social Security program, and HI stands for Hospital Insurance (Medicare).

Social Security

	Tax rates as a percent of taxable earnings					
	Rate for employees and employers, each			Rate for self-employed workers		
Year	OASDI	HI	Total	OASDI	HI	Total
1937-49	1.000	–	1.000	–	–	–
1950	1.500	–	1.500	–	–	–
1951-53	1.500	–	1.500	2.250	–	2.250
1954-56	2.000	–	2.000	3.000	–	3.000
1957-58	2.250	–	2.250	3.375	–	3.375
1959	2.500	–	2.500	3.750	–	3.750
1960-61	3.000	–	3.000	4.500	–	4.500
1962	3.125	–	3.125	4.700	–	4.700
1963-65	3.625	–	3.625	5.400	–	5.400
1966	3.850	0.350	4.200	5.800	0.350	6.150
1967	3.900	0.500	4.400	5.900	0.500	6.400
1968	3.800	0.600	4.400	5.800	0.600	6.400
1969-70	4.200	0.600	4.800	6.300	0.600	6.900
1971-72	4.600	0.600	5.200	6.900	0.600	7.500
1973	4.850	1.000	5.850	7.000	1.000	8.000
1974-77	4.950	0.900	5.850	7.000	0.900	7.900
1978	5.050	1.000	6.050	7.100	1.000	8.100
1979-80	5.080	1.050	6.130	7.050	1.050	8.100
1981	5.350	1.300	6.650	8.000	1.300	9.300
1982-83	5.400	1.300	6.700	8.050	1.300	9.350
1984 [a]	5.700	1.300	7.000	11.400	2.600	14.000
1985 [a]	5.700	1.350	7.050	11.400	2.700	14.100
1986-87 [a]	5.700	1.450	7.150	11.400	2.900	14.300

Year	Tax rates as a percent of taxable earnings					
	Rate for employees and employers, each			Rate for self-employed workers		
	OASDI	HI	Total	OASDI	HI	Total
1988-89 [a]	6.060	1.450	7.510	12.120	2.900	15.020
1990 and later [b], [c]	6.200	1.450	7.650	12.400	2.900	15.300

[a] In 1984 only, an immediate credit of 0.3 percent of taxable wages was allowed against the OASDI taxes paid by employees, resulting in an effective employee tax rate of 5.4 percent. The OASI and DI trust funds, however, received general revenue equivalent to 0.3 percent of taxable wages for 1984. Similar credits of 2.7 percent, 2.3 percent, and 2.0 percent were allowed against the combined OASDI and HI taxes on net earnings from self-employment in 1984, 1985, and 1986-89, respectively.

[b] Beginning in 1990, self-employed workers are allowed a deduction, for purposes of computing their net earnings, equal to half of the combined OASDI and HI contributions that would be payable without regard to the contribution and benefit base. The OASDI contribution rate is then applied to net earnings after this deduction, but subject to the OASDI base.

[c] For 2010, most employers were exempt from paying the employer share of OASDI tax on wages paid to certain qualified individuals hired after February 3. For 2011, the OASDI tax rate is reduced by 2 percentage points for employees and for self-employed workers, resulting in a 4.2 percent effective tax rate for employees and a 10.4 percent effective tax rate for self-employed workers. The reductions in 2010 and 2011 tax revenue due to lower tax rates will be made up by transfers from the general fund of the Treasury to the OASI and DI trust funds. Beginning in 2013, an additional HI tax of 0.9 percent is assessed on earned income exceeding $200,000 for individuals and $250,000 for married couples filing jointly. This additional HI tax rate is *not* reflected in the tax rates shown in the table.

Increase of Income Limit for Payroll Tax

An increase in the income limit for payroll taxes is a highly likely scenario. Such a move would increase the amount of income that is subject to the tax described above. Not all income is subject to OASDI tax, only the first $106,800 in 2011. This figure adjusts each year along with what's called the National Average Wage Index and is scheduled to increase to $110,100 in 2012. As an example, someone earning over $106,800 in 2011 would pay 4.2% or $4,485.60 in tax for the privilege of all the benefits Social Security provides, and the person's employer would pay 6.2% (Congress did not extend the payroll tax cut to employers) for a total amount of $11,107.20. Normally, per the table above, they would pay 6.2% each, which totals $13,243.20. This sounds like a lot of money, and it is. However, actuarially (the business of crunching numbers related to longevity) it isn't enough to pay out the level of benefits Social Security does when considering disability income, survivor's benefits, and of course, longer retirement periods than anyone imagined. It cannot increase faster than the National Average Wage Index under current rules, but Congress can change the rules.

They could decide that this same percentage tax applies to all income up to $200,000. Using the same tax rates, this would result in $24,800 of tax due in exchange for Social Security's benefits. This proposal has one intriguing quality to it, and several major disadvantages.

The motivation behind this option is that the tax is what's called regressive. This means that as someone earns more income, this tax, as a percentage of the total, actually goes down due to the cap. For example, if a worker earns $75,000 and pays 6.2% of this income in FICA tax, the percentage of the total is obviously 6.2%. However, let's say another worker earns $250,000 and pays 6.2% on the first 106,800, or $6,621.60. But how much of their total income as a percentage did they pay? If we divide $6,621.60 by $250,000, we get 2.6%, a much lower percentage. Therefore, as someone earns more and more income, the tax is said to regress as a percentage of the total.

Some argue that this is unfair and that either the tax should increase as one moves up the taxable income ladder or a higher portion of the income should be taxed at the 6.2% rate or whatever rate is in effect at the time. Studies done by Social Security actuaries have shown that by removing the income cap entirely Social Security would be on a solid financial foundation going out beyond 80 years—in other words, indefinitely. Before we jump for joy, however, for having solved the nation's old-age security problem, we need to account for the huge negative ramifications removing the income cap would cause.

Such a change would reduce employees' spendable income dramatically. Someone earning $200,000 would have $5,778.40 or about $500 every month less to spend on goods and services. You may be thinking, "Well, they make $200,000," but we're considering how this affects the overall economy, not one particular person's finances. If you take away $6,000 a year from every household in America earning $200,000, it could immediately put the country into a damaging recession.

Earnings of $200,000 may sound like a lot, but in this great country of ours there are millions of households managing to do it. Worse yet, the employer paying these wages would have this same tax increase. Think of the small business that has 10 workers, out of 50 making over $106,800. For those 10 workers, the business has to pay possibly thousands of dollars each for a benefit it will never see anything from. Businesses don't get Social Security when they retire, but they have to pay Social Security taxes on the employee's behalf. But what if the business owner says, "Well, if I lay off one or two of those people I'll break even and can continue as I am now. The other staff will just have to pick up the slack"? And that's precisely what thousands of business owners could do, resulting in a monumental increase in unemployment. The current levels of taxes are actually one of the reasons our economy is slower this time around to recover and slower to hire additional help than in previous recoveries from recessions. The cost to an employer isn't just the salary. It is health insurance, other benefits, and the employer portion of the OASDI tax all added together, plus time training them and so on.

With that said, an increase in the wage limit that is phased in could be down the road as the country faces a shorter time frame in which to act on Social Security's exceedingly real problems. The key here for those looking to make intelligent financial planning decisions is to keep the perceived problems in perspective. Social Security's benefits to the average citizen are extraordinary when considered in light of the history of national employee pension systems and when compared to the pension systems of many other countries. Take action with your local congressperson if you feel strongly one way or another about taxes.

Retirement Age

The most likely change, in my opinion, would be a gradual adjustment to the age at which recipients can begin to receive payments, and the age at which someone is deemed to have reached "full retirement." The proposals range from increasing full retirement age from 67 to age 70 for those born prior to 1960, with corresponding increases for people born in other years, to increasing the age one can begin receiving payments from 62 to 65 and beyond, or a combination of the two.

Let's take a step back, though, and look at why it makes sense that Congress would choose this strategy as a way to increase the viability of the system. Social Security began in 1937 with monthly benefits officially starting in 1940. At that time, a person needed to be 65 to receive benefits. There was no age 62 provision, because it wasn't enacted until 1956. A person 65 years old in 1940 had an average life expectancy of 12.7 years from that point forward. So if they made it to 65, they had a chance on average to live another decade or so. Now, as of 2001, according to the National Association of Insurance Commissioners, a male's life expectancy once they reach age 65 is 16.8 additional years and a female's life expectancy is 20.1 years. Many of these people may have already started receiving benefits years earlier, at age 62. This means for every decade that goes by, a person has an average life expectancy of one year longer, starting from the same point of age 65. That is wonderful news for all of us, with the exception that Social Security hasn't adjusted along with it. In fact, it has reduced the age one needs to reach to receive benefits through the provision of early benefits.

In 1983, amendments were made to Social Security to increase the full retirement age to its current table, which follows.

Year of Birth*	Full Retirement Age
1937 or earlier	65
1938	65 and 2 months
1939	65 and 4 months
1940	65 and 6 months
1941	65 and 8 months
1942	65 and 10 months
1943-1954	66
1955	66 and 2 months
1956	66 and 4 months
1957	66 and 6 months
1958	66 and 8 months
1959	66 and 10 months
1960 and later	67

If you were born on January 1st of any year you should refer to the previous year.

Source: http://www.ssa.gov

It has been 38 years since that last adjustment. Many young people have grown up accustomed to the idea that they won't get Social Security anyway. People are living a lot longer than they have in the past, and medical advances are expected to keep increasing life expectancy. To remedy the system while alienating the fewest possible voters, and using medical advances as the reasoning, seems like a politically perfect storm for some future Congress. This explanation isn't meant to convey what would work the best, or what your author would be most in favor of, but rather to simply outline what seems politically most likely given history and the current environment in Washington.

What to Do for the Rest of Us

Unless you are under the CSRS, the benefits of Social Security are the same whether you worked for the federal government or in the private sector. FERS employees, those who began work for the federal government after 1984, receive a pension in addition to Social Security and in many cases find that it can add up to enough to cover a household's monthly bills, especially if you have done some planning ahead of time to limit those expenses as much as possible.

For those in the private sector, it's all the more important to use Social Security to its full potential. Make sure your earnings credits are correct, check with your local office if a major event occurs like a birth, death, disability, or divorce to see what's available. Also, keep your annual benefit statements or go online to estimate your benefit. You may be surprised by how much it is. And if you are anywhere near retirement and keep in touch with your congressman, you will still probably get something out of Social Security. You never know, it may even be enough, along with some other savings, to punch out from work for the last time.

CHAPTER 6

Health Insurance

John was 58. He said, "I've done everything that was needed to be done, and everything the financial planning books asked me to. I saved my money. I took risk in the markets to get it to grow but kept it diversified. When the market took a downturn I took a hit but not as much as some people I talked to. I've almost paid the house off, and my daughter only has one semester left of college. The only mortgage is actually the equity line I took out to help her pay for school."

John had been at the same company for 25 years. He just kept going and they always had a project that needed to get done.

This chapter summarizes the basics of the federal health insurance program and examines some general advantages compared to the private sector. Due to the enormous complexity and rapidly changing nature of our health care system today, to provide guidance requires a close evaluation of an individual's situation.

The recurring theme here has been to simply ask questions, even ones that seem obvious or dumb. And the best advice is really what the doctor has been saying, "Just try to stay healthy."

John continued, "I was fortunate that the company stayed in business that long. It wasn't really my dream job, though, and 25 years is a long time. What I would really like to do is volunteer or work for an organization promoting sustainable environmental practices. It can't really be a career, though, because I don't have any experience and don't want to work full time.

"I just know it's something I'm passionate about and want to get involved. I have enough money set aside to get me to Social Security age, and my assets can produce enough income to get by supplementing the payment I will get from that. The only bills I really have are my utilities, telephone, food, and property taxes. I will tell you though, none of those come close to what I would have to pay for health insurance if I retired.

"My company pays for it now and thank goodness they do. I was talking to human resources the other day and they said if I had to pay it myself it would cost about a thousand dollars a month! I can't afford that. I asked them what else I can do and they explained to me the process of COBRA, but that only lasts 18 months. I don't know if I can even get coverage after that.

"What am I supposed to do from 60 to 65 when I get to Medicare? A friend of mine was saying there are these programs I can use from the state but it's so confusing and the cost is the same, like a thousand a month. I can't go without health insurance. That would be crazy with the prescriptions I'm taking. I would end up paying more, and what if something happens?

"How did people do it years ago? I guess they just didn't have medical care to worry about, or their employer took care of them. I really don't want to work another five to seven more years, but unless I accumulate a lot more money to use to pay for it, or the cost goes down, I'm out of luck. And it doesn't seem like either of those things are going to happen anytime soon."

The Federal Employee Health Benefits plan (FEHB) is the largest employer-sponsored group health plan in the world. It offers access to health insurance, vision, dental, prescription drug, and health savings accounts, among other health-related provisions.

Participants can choose between more affordable HMO plans all the way up to comprehensive and flexible PPO coverage. There are seminars, human resource contacts, and handbooks available to assist in making the tough decisions. The government pays for a large portion (approximately 72%) of the cost of the coverage, and while you are working and when you retire the premiums can be automatically taken out of your pension regardless of the age that you retire, provided you qualify to keep FEHB coverage. When you reach age 65 you can switch to Medicare Part B, or keep your current coverage depending on your customized family and medical circumstances. Review the plan options thoroughly however cancelling FEHB may not be the best choice. With health costs these days it provides a great deal of peace of mind to know that no matter what happens your employment qualifies you for the best health care money can buy. Let's take a closer look.

Eligibility

FEHB is open to any federal employee and their family unless their position is specifically excluded by law. These laws do not affect many workers, with the notable exception of those of a temporary status. If you don't enroll within 60 days of becoming eligible when you are hired, then you can enroll and/or change your coverage during the annual enrollment period (in November/December of each year), you can provide medical information in order to qualify for the coverage, or you can experience a qualifying life event. These include things like marriage, death, divorce, and births. An excellent resource for FEHB, and a breakdown of the entire program, is available at the following website: http://www.opm.gov/insure/federal_employ/index.asp.

Enrollment

During enrollment at date of hire, or open season near the end of each year you have the option of several different forms of health coverage. These are referred to by acronyms like PPO, HMO, FFS, and POS, among others. The differences can get confusing but generally apply to whether the provider of the care is in the plan network or not.

Check with the plan, though, and ask questions to make sure you are getting the best deal. To further research this, contact the plan to ask if your doctors, specialists, and even the hospital you would probably be taken to if there was an emergency are part of the network. There's always the chance that this information isn't accurate, however, so check with your doctors personally as well. If you are already enrolled in a plan and need to see a specialist, contact them to see if they are part of the network. They will be able to find out. The customer service contacts at doctors' offices are invaluable resources in understanding the language that health insurance companies speak, and in figuring how to get things done.

Cost

Here's the great part of the government plan. When you enroll there is a cost, of course. However, whether you choose a top-of-the-line plan, and whether you enroll your family or just yourself, the government, as your employer, will cover approximately 72% of the cost of the premium. For an example, in Maryland a plan for a family provided by the carrier Aetna that is open access, meaning there is the option of going out of network, costs $1,165.13 per month, but after a government subsidy the total monthly cost to the employee is $291.28. Not a bad rate for family coverage without having a high deductible. This is just one example and is subject to change over time, so again, check with HR to get all your questions answered if you are signing up for a particular plan. A nationwide popular Blue Cross Blue Shield program is also available among many others. The $291.28 is paid through payroll deduction and comes out pre-tax, so you get a deduction off of your taxable income for paying the premium. This tax benefit goes away at retirement, so while the premium itself does not go up just because you retire, you will have an increased tax burden on that amount of income when you retire.

Health Savings Accounts

A popular way to contain costs in the federal program and across the country is through the use of Health Savings Accounts (HSA). This process is easier than it seems and a fantastic option for a healthy family that doesn't expect to use much of their health benefits. In exchange for a higher deductible, a member will enjoy noticeably lower out-of-pocket costs and the opportunity to deposit pre-tax dollars in an account for later use. These funds can be invested for growth and do not go away at the end of the plan year, as is the case with flexible spending accounts. You are limited as to how much you can contribute to a HSA in a tax year to the following:

> Individual coverage - $3,100
> Family coverage - $6,250

Once the money is in this account, it grows tax-free and if it is used for qualified medical expenses the distribution can come at any time and is tax-free at that time as well. It gets better. Once you turn age 65, if there are funds in your HSA you can begin to use them for non-medical expenses and there is no penalty for distribution. You do pay income tax on the distribution if you don't use it for medical expenses.

Imagine accumulating enough money in your health savings account by age 65 that you could pick and choose whether to pay income tax depending on the particular expense, and never have required distributions or tax on any gains over time. To get started you need to have the cash flow to start contributing to the HSA. But what if you don't have it? That's why you switched to the plan in the first place, to save money. In 2006 they came out with an option where you can directly transfer money from an IRA, into the HSA. This limit is the amount of your contribution limit above, depending on your coverage type. This takes up to $6,250 from an account that is taxable to access, with a 10% penalty if access occurs prior to age 59.5, and makes it entirely tax-free to take any time if a medical expenses comes up, and only taxable as income a few years later at age

65. There are rules to make sure you qualify, such as staying in the high-deductible health plan for a full 12 months following the transfer, and not taking receipt of the funds in the process at any point, so check with a tax advisor and your plan sponsor to make sure you do it correctly. Also, if you have the funds available just fund the HSA directly and keep your IRA money growing. But if you don't have the funds available, then this may be a good option to give you a head start.

All of this presumes you work for an employer that offers a high-deductible plan as an option. Although the number of employers who offer this type of plan is growing quickly, many employers don't provide this plan yet. If you work for the federal government, however, you can choose it, and if you're not expecting too many health-related bills in the near future, it may make sense.

Resources

Each health insurance company has come out with their own website that is designed to provide customized information for members of the federal plan. There is the following site for those who choose CareFirst:

> http://www.fepblue.org

For members of Aetna, there is the following site:

> http://custom.aetna.com/fehbp/index.php

Other companies have their own sites:

http://www.opm.gov/insure/health/planinfo/index.asp

There are also workshops on getting the most out of your benefits, smoking cessation programs, and regular correspondence. And some institutions offer other programs, including USALearning and Grantham University.

Conversion upon Retirement

Once you are eligible to retire from federal employment and choose to do so, you can convert your health coverage into retiree health care, and all of its features continue. This can occur regardless of your age at retirement as long as you have met the requirements to retire from federal service. The employer contribution toward your health coverage is the same, and is simply deducted from your annuity every month. If there is a death, the other family members under the plan may continue the coverage if it's a spouse who was entitled to spousal annuity payments. This is important for those interested in exploring a planning option where life insurance is purchased in place of a survivorship provision. See a financial planner regarding this concept. At age 65 you can sign up for Medicare, and generally it would become your primary health coverage with FEHB becoming your secondary health coverage. In retirement, however your premiums are not pre-tax, so they will be higher.

Medicare A

Everyone is eligible for Medicare, not just federal employees, so let's look at some of the main provisions it offers.

At age 65, whether you have elected Social Security or not, Medicare A is automatically available to you and is free, provided you or a spouse worked for 10 years in Medicare-eligible employment. Be sure to sign up as soon after reaching age 65 as you can. Otherwise enrollment can be delayed. A wealth of information is available about Medicare at the following website:

http://www.Medicare.gov

You should explore the Medicare website if you are close to age 65 in order to familiarize yourself with the services available. Also contact your medical providers, your doctors and specialists, and tell them you are going to enroll. Ask them what to expect and how the benefits will affect their services.

Part A is hospital insurance. It covers inpatient care and some forms of skilled nursing care, but the latter only on a temporary basis. If you have a three-day-and-night stay in a hospital due to your condition, you require skilled care rather than custodial care, and you show continual improvement, Medicare will cover all of the costs for the first 20 days and some of the cost for the next 80 days.

After that, as discussed in Chapter 3, you either are on your own or your long-term care insurance will need to kick in. As stated, Part A is free, but only because during your working years taxes were paid out of your wages and by your employer. The current tax rate for Medicare is 1.45% on all wages by both employee and employer, totaling 2.9%. There is no income cap on Medicare taxes as there is on Social Security. So if you earn $1,000,000, you and your employer combined would pay $29,000. Taxes for Medicare began in 1966 at 0.35% each and have been 1.45% each since 1986.

Medicare B

In addition to Part A, some people sign up for Part B, which covers preventative services. The following table lists these services and the annual deductible that applies.

Health Insurance

Part B Services

Services	You pay
Part B Deductible	You pay: $140 per year.
Blood	In most cases, the provider gets blood from a blood bank at no charge, and you won't have to pay for it or replace it. However, you will pay a copayment for the blood processing and handling services for every unit of blood you get, and the Part B deductible applies. If the provider has to buy blood for you, you must either pay the provider costs for the first 3 units of blood you get in a calendar year or have the blood donated by you or someone else. You pay a copayment for additional units of blood you get as an outpatient (after the first 3), and the Part B deductible applies.
Clinical Laboratory Services	You pay: $0 for Medicare-approved services.
Home Health Services	You pay: $0 for Medicare-approved services. You pay 20% of the Medicare-approved amount for durable medical equipment.
Medical and Other Services	You pay: 20% of the Medicare-approved amount for most doctor services (including most doctor services while you're a hospital inpatient), outpatient therapy,* and durable medical equipment.
Mental Health Services	You pay: 40% of the Medicare-approved amount for most outpatient mental health care.
Other Covered Services	You pay: copayment or coinsurance amounts.
Outpatient Hospital Services	You pay: a coinsurance (for doctor services) or a copayment amount for most outpatient hospital services. The copayment for a single service can't be more than the amount of the inpatient hospital deductible.

Source: http://www.Medicare.gov

There is a cost for Part B, and it is based on your retirement income. It is, however, a favorable schedule compared to premiums for younger people and is graduated liberally to where most households will pay the minimum amount. Those earning less than $170,000 as a joint filer will pay $99.90 monthly per person. If you have a good year from an income standpoint your Medicare Part B premiums will be adjusted for the entire following year. This can happen from unusual transactions like large IRA distributions, the sale of a property or business, or the sale of an appreciated stock.

So a tip would be, if you can control it, try and limit any of these events to totaling, along with your regular income, under $170,000. Keep in mind, though, that even if it does reach up to $319,000, for example, your Medicare premiums will increase just $100 a month for only the following year. A $100 increase is a noticeable one, but its temporary, and hopefully you have some of that increased income set aside. All of this assumes you sign up on time. The penalty for not signing up for Part B is more costly than waiting on Part A, because the monthly fee increases. For every year you are eligible for Part B and don't sign up, the monthly premium increases by 10% and stays higher for the rest of your life.

If you were eligible in 2009 and you waited until 2011 to enroll, you would pay 20% more than the figures shown in the following table for the same coverage. That can add up to a lot of money, so plan ahead of time and decide which form of coverage you will take prior to turning 65.

If Your Yearly Income in 2010 was		You pay
File Individual Tax Return	Joint Tax Return	Monthly
$85,000 or less	$170,000 or less	$99.90
above $85,001 up to $107,000	above $170,001 up to $214,000	$139.90
above $107,001 up to $160,000	above $214,001 up to $320,000	$199.80
above $160,001 up to $214,000	above $320,001 up to $428,000	$259.70
above $214,000	above $428,000	$319.70

Source: http://www.Medicare.gov

Medicare C

This is where it can get confusing. In 1997, with the Balanced Budget Act, Medicare participants were given the option of using private health insurance, similar to what is offered through an employer. Members could choose between HMO, PPO, and even plans that include a medical savings account like an HSA. In 2003, these plans were expanded to include drug coverage. It is referred to as Part C, Medicare Choice, or Medicare Advantage plans. These all generally refer to the same thing. They offer more comprehensive health insurance than Part A and B alone and include dental and vision as well as wellness programs.

There is a fee for this option in addition to the Part B premium because both work together to provide the care. Because this plan is offered by private insurance companies, there is not a stated fee per month. It depends on the level of coverage and the geographic area the person lives in. Medigap, an alternative to private Part C coverage, is still around and used by many beneficiaries as a way to obtain supplemental health coverage directly from Medicare rather than the private insurance companies. It isn't clear-cut whether Part C or Medigap is better, because that will depend on your particular needs. The key is to know that these plans are generally interchangeable and to ask questions of your health care providers to determine the best choice in your case.

If you live in a densely populated area, there should a practitioner of every major medical specialty relatively close by who accepts the health coverage you have or may purchase in the future. Plan ahead, acknowledge that a health event may happen, and do the research. Another great resource is simply contacting Medicare directly at 1-800-MEDICARE or 1-800-633-4227. Your family will thank you, and there will be fewer surprises as you get older.

Medicare D

To obtain prescription drug coverage as a senior, you may either sign up for Medicare Part D or get drug coverage through a privately offered health plan that includes prescriptions in its benefits. When picking a drug plan, most people are already on certain medications, so picking a plan for this type of coverage can be easier because you know what drugs need to be covered right away. Medicare provides the following table to assist you when choosing a plan.

If you...	You might want to...
... currently take specific prescription drugs.	...look for plans that offer coverage in the coverage gap, and then check with those plans to be sure your drugs would be covered during the gap. (These plans may charge a higher monthly premium.)
...want your drug expenses to be balanced throughout the year.	...look at plans with low or no deductibles.

If you...	You might want to...
...use a lot of generic prescriptions.	...look at plans with tiers that charge you nothing or low copayments for generic prescriptions.
...don't have many drug costs now, but want coverage for peace of mind and to avoid future penalties	...look for plans with low monthly premiums for drug coverage. If you need prescriptions in the future, all plans still must cover most drugs used by people with Medicare.
...like the extra benefits and lower costs that you might get by getting your health care and prescription drug coverage from one plan and are willing to accept the plan's restrictions on what doctors, hospitals, and other medical providers you can use.	...look for Medicare Advantage Plans with prescription drug coverage.

Source: http://www.medicare.gov/Publications/Pubs/pdf/11163.pdf

There is discussion in this table, as well as a majority of the time Part D comes up, about the "coverage gap" that is referred to as the "Donut Hole." This is a term used to describe a possible temporary loss of coverage for prescription drugs depending on the plan you have, costing in some cases several thousand dollars a year in addition to your monthly premium. Thankfully, the donut hole doesn't have to be something that comes as a surprise provided you understand how it can arise.

In addition, as part of the massive new health care bill which we will cover next, starting in 2011 plans began a gradual phase-out of the donut hole possibility that will be completed by 2020. So after this point, participants won't have to worry about these increased costs and will see a reduction of the cost between now and then.

Essentially, there is a dollar limit that is tracked regarding spending on prescription drugs between the insurance company and your actual costs. In 2011 this level was approximately $2,930, depending the specific plan you have. Again, this doesn't represent how much you would pay, but rather you and the insurance company combined. So if there is a prescription that costs you $20 and the insurance company $100, $120 would be applied. Once you reached this level you would have to cover 100% of the cost of your prescription costs until your personal (not including the insurance company) payments totaled $4,700 in that year.

At this point, "catastrophic coverage" would kick in and cover costs going forward. This can add up to a lot of money for a senior every year, and not for a product they can just choose to forgo. Let's say $500 of the first $2,930 was the person's cost, and the rest was covered by the insurance company. That would mean of the first $4,700 in drug costs in a given year (not that difficult to reach these days), $2,270 could be entirely out of pocket. This means all of the first $500 and all of the difference between $4,700 and $2,930 or $1,770. Starting in 2011 and each year going forward until 2020, participants will receive discounts on purchases made during the coverage gap starting at around 50% of the cost. In addition, in 2010 all participants, when they entered the donut hole, received a tax-free $250 rebate check.

New National Health Care Law

Entire books are written about the various subjects discussed in this chapter. The amount of information and planning around those options is endless. However, due to our constantly changing health care scene it's equally important to cover how it could change, rather than just how it currently works. In 2010 President Obama signed the Patient Protection and Affordable Care Act (PPACA). This is a huge law that covers practically all aspects of health care delivered today. A thorough resource on it and the timeline for its implementation are available at the following website:

http://www.healthcare.gov

Some of the key features of the new law are the ability to receive health insurance if you have a preexisting condition, tax credits for small businesses to offer early retiree health coverage, and limits in the ability of insurance companies to place an annual or lifetime limit on how much they will pay out in benefits for a single beneficiary.

There is a phase-in of these provisions and many more that will occur through 2014, however, numerous court battles are ongoing to determine the constitutionality of various provisions of the law. The most contentious of these disagreements comes from the individual states that are arguing against requiring their citizens to obtain health coverage and objecting to the additional burden it places on them to carry out other portions of the law.

What to Do for the Rest of Us

The best defense is a good offense. The only thing about health care you can attempt to control is how little you have to use it. And from a financial standpoint maintaining a healthy body and mind may be one of the most lucrative decisions you make in your life. It doesn't come up too often in a financial planning session, but if a comprehensive strategy is really the goal, looking at health-related costs is something that really needs to be done.

I'm not a doctor and could never be one given my embarrassing response to the sight of blood; however, I'm a big fan of Dr. Mehmet Oz. If you have never heard of him, you should check out his books and TV show. He's made a career out of explaining health concepts in an easy-to-understand way and offering implementable strategies to improve one's health. A list of some of them is as follows, summarized from his and Dr. Michael Roizen's book *You: Staying Young: The Owner's*

Manual for Extending Your Warranty. Show the following points to your doctor and see what he or she says:

1. Get moderate exercise at least a few times a week. It gets your heart rate up and builds muscles.
2. Floss daily. Through your mouth is one of the main ways bacteria gets into your body.
3. Take the correct vitamins, per your doctor's recommendations.
4. Get the tests your sex and age determine as soon as you are supposed to.
5. Be a lifelong learner. Constantly try new hobbies and activities. It exercises your brain.
6. Have a plan to fight stress. Try yoga, or other stress reduction techniques, and have an open line of communication with friends and family.
7. Enjoy life. Keep in touch with friends and family and try to laugh as much as possible.
8. Get sleep. Try to get at least seven hours a night. There are many tips in the book to help you sleep better.
9. Eat as much fresh food as possible. Fruits, vegetables, grains, and water.
10. Quit smoking as soon as possible.
11. Know your family history. Find out as much as you can about the lifelong health and conditions that affected your parents and grandparents and make sure the information gets into your doctor's file.
12. Keep an eye on your weight. Always the most difficult thing to do, but if you can at least consistently keep track of what's called your BMI, it will help you maintain a healthy weight.

The book is a few hundred pages and is just one of several books from Drs. Oz and Roizen, so this obviously isn't meant as an all-encompassing list. He does also choose to promote a wide variety of natural remedies that some doctors feel don't actually provide any assistance, but the key is following the information out there and keeping current on what may benefit you. If you stick with this, keep in touch with your doctors and family, stay consistent, and understand the programs available, you should be ahead of the game.

CHAPTER 7

FEGLI/Life Insurance

This chapter explains the federal life insurance programs and their variety of options. Like the pension provision, the government's life insurance offering is noticeably different from what you will typically find in the private sector. For those in the private sector, coverage is certainly still available depending on your insurability. It does involve, however, the use of an insurance agent who can lay out a few different options for you.

Adam knew he needed life insurance. "I have a wife, two kids, another on the way and a mortgage," he said.

"I have no idea what Ellen would do if I died," Adam said. I don't know what took me so long to try and figure out how to handle it, either. I guess I just didn't want to think about it. Who wants to plan out how a large pile of money is going to be spent by someone other than yourself, who only has it because you're dead?" he said chuckling. "And you get the joy of trying to work it into the budget for that privilege."

There was a problem, though. Adam had gotten around to going through the process of getting the insurance. He filled out an application, and he went through the exam process. The insurance company doesn't just give the coverage away; there has to be an approval. He was 37 and figured he would be just fine. He had a stable job now at the State Department, and the premiums weren't that much based on the quote he got from his financial planner. They had just met, and it was of the first things they decided needed to be covered.

But then he got the call. John, his financial planner, contacted Adam and Ellen to make an appointment to sit down and talk. When they got to John's office, John said, "We got the word back from the insurance company. I'm sorry to tell you they said they won't be able to offer coverage. I don't know all the details because they keep the medical information as private as possible. They said it had something to do with the blood work. Now, I have a letter here you can sign to get a copy of the blood work. And the next step really is to wait for that and show it to your doctor. They'll know how to interpret the numbers and will explain the next step." Adam was confused. He didn't go the doctor other than the one time he had broken his wrist playing basketball and another when he had the flu. "I'm fine. I'm in good health. What do I do now?" John told him to just be patient.

"We need to take this one step at a time," John said. "I'll send this letter asking for the blood-work documentation, and when you get the mailing from the insurance company take it to your doctor and let me know."

A couple of weeks later John and Adam talked. "They said I have a non-terminal condition," Adam said. "Thank goodness I went through this process. There is treatment for it, which I've started. My doctor would only have known about it through blood work, but there was never a reason to do that."

John took that information and did a little research, but it was the same result across the board from other insurance companies until things were well under control which could be a year or more. "All right," he told Adam, "the next step is to go see human resources at your office. We need to increase your group life through work as much as we can. I was hoping you could save some money by getting a good rating with the private coverage or at least customize it to what you are specifically looking for. Thankfully, you work for the government. I don't know if you know this, but you're entitled to $528,000 worth of life insurance through them. The first $128,000 of it is practically free, and the other $400,000 is five times your salary, which you will pay for—but it's competitively priced. Let's get it when you can. It's less in face amount than we applied for in the private market, but it's a start. You can keep in touch with your doctor and let me know how your health progresses. You will be able to sign up either at the next open enrollment, or when your son is born they offer you a special opportunity to add some coverage".

Adam said, "That's great! That's a lot of money." Adam and Ellen know they should have made arrangements for him to get life insurance much sooner. Fortunately, things turned out all right. They were able to get his condition under control, and he set up a regimen of doctor's visits and prescriptions. The peace of mind that half a million dollars in coverage provided, though, was invaluable.

Most families spend more time debating the merits of various cable TV bundles than they do their life insurance choices. Life insurance can be a powerful thing. It can guarantee a legacy, provide peace of mind, cover estate taxes, act as a savings account, and if paid out, protect the livelihood of beneficiaries. All of those goals can even be accomplished with one policy, if desired. Sometimes life insurance isn't purchased due to the cost. People don't want to pay for something they don't believe will happen and not get anything back when they prove themselves right by surviving beyond the term of the policy.

According to LIMRA's (Life Insurance and Market Research Association) 2011 study, only one-third of individuals are covered by life insurance, and the average amount in force was $154,000. This is the lowest level in our country in fifty years. Only 56% of workers had group life insurance through their employers, and on average this insurance was $102,300 in death benefits. We will walk through a calculation to determine how to estimate the required amount of insurance for a typical household, but the figure just mentioned is obviously not enough.

Federal employees are entitled to enroll at certain times in a program called Federal Employees' Group Life Insurance (FEGLI). This program was established in 1954, and with its coverage of four million people it is the largest group life insurance program in the world. Within the program, there is the Basic coverage and then Options A, B, and C. Basic coverage equals annual base pay plus $2,000, or $10,000, whichever is greater. For those age 35 and under, this amount is doubled at no extra charge. Starting at age 36, the amount reduces by 10% down to its standard amount of one times base pay, by age 45. The Basic coverage is automatic (if not waived), and there is then the option of taking one or more of the supplemental insurance choices (Options A, B and/or C).

Option A, the standard additional coverage, adds $10,000 of life insurance to the total. Option B, optional additional coverage, is the most important for planning purposes. This option offers the opportunity for employees to secure up to five times their salary in additional life insurance. Even better, no underwriting is required, so the insurance is available regardless of your health at the time of enrollment provided you sign up when you become employed. Annually, the amount of the coverage will increase as pay raises are earned. Lastly, Option C allows spousal and dependent coverage for the employee's family. It may be purchased in $5,000 increments up to $25,000 for a spouse and in $2,500 increments up to $12,500 for each dependent child. This is usually considered burial insurance for the family members covered. The average cost of a funeral in 2012 was approximately $7,755. For most folks that's a lot of money, and during a time of bereavement having to use up savings adds an unnecessary level of stress.

None of these coverage options are free. There is a separate cost for all of them. The Basic coverage is subsidized by the government, which pays one-third of the total cost. The full cost of each of the other options is borne by the employee. The Office of Personnel Management (OPM) offers an extensive calculator to determine the cost of each household's preferred insurance options at the following website:

http://www.opm.gov/calculator/check.asp

This calculator reflects premium adjustments made in November 2011 after they had remained static since 2005. In some cases, such as Option B, and for younger enrollees in Option C, premiums actually decreased. For age bands above age 45, premiums mostly increased slightly. As an example of the cost of this coverage, we will look at the recently updated table for Option B, which follows. The cost is per $1,000 of death benefit. Keep in mind this is the cost while employed. Once retired it changes depending on which type and how much coverage you keep.

Age Band	Biweekly	Monthly
Under 35	$0.02	$0.043
35-39	$0.03	$0.065
40-44	$0.05	$0.108
45-49	$0.08	$0.173
50-54	$0.13	$0.282
55-59	$0.23	$.0498
60-64	$0.52	$1.127
65-69	$0.62	$1.343
70-74	$1.14	$2.470
75-79	$1.80	$3.900
80 and over	$2.40	$5.200

Using the figures in this table as a guide, we can estimate a sample of the biweekly premium for a given employee. If a 50-year-old male has an annual salary of $80,000 and chooses to purchase the full multiple of five times his salary, he would purchase $400,000 of coverage from Option B alone. He is purchasing 400 units of coverage at $0.282 per unit, or $112.80 per month, if payroll is on a monthly basis for the enrollee. Let's assume he is paid monthly for a moment in order to compare the cost to the private marketplace. This price is within the range of term life insurance costs of the private marketplace, depending on one's health. Using quotes from Banner Life, a life insurance company that is A+ rated from A.M. Best a financial strength ratings company, a $400,000 15-level term life policy would cost a standard non-tobacco user $108.59 a month. A 15-year term is used here under the assumption that the 50-year-old will work to his approximate normal retirement age of 65, or 15 additional years, and would want to keep the insurance in force during this term.

The difference between the government's Option B and the Banner Life policy goes well beyond initial cost, however. A significant advantage of obtaining coverage in the private marketplace is that the cost remains the same during the term of the policy. So this Banner Life policy has a level cost over the entire 15-year term, while the cost of group life coverage through the government, or any employer arrangement, increases as the employee gets older.

Another aspect of group life that may be positive or negative is the lack of underwriting required to sign up provided you do so when you are hired. If enrollees are healthy, they can receive a significant discount on a private policy, while if they have one or more of several conditions, or smoke, FEGLI will be the deal of lifetime. To give an example, the same private term life policy quoted earlier would only cost $63.09 a month ($630 annual savings) provided the insured received a preferred health rating. This generally means they are taking few to no medications, have no major health events in the past, and have good family history, although all insurance company underwriting guidelines are unique, including those of the company quoted here. On the other end of the spectrum would be smoker rates. If you ever needed another reason to quit smoking, here it is, or at least a reason to get a job with the federal government so you can get group rates on your life insurance. For the same private policy, a $400,000 15-year level term policy for a 50-year-old male, but with smoker rates, the monthly cost becomes $277.64. The FEGLI rates don't distinguish between smoker and non-smoker, so the same $112.80 monthly premium would apply, for an annual savings to this particular enrollee of $1,978.08.

FEGLI has another advantage, but it doesn't have anything to do with the nominal cost of the coverage. When working with individuals in a financial planning environment, there are certain "human nature" tendencies that come out. No one likes discussing a bill. They think, "Don't I have enough of those already?" Or, "I can't afford that," even if we've already discussed a budget. That's life.

Taking on a required payment every single month can be daunting. So what's the solution? Take it out of your paycheck before you ever see it. This one step has helped the 401(k) industry grow to a trillion-dollar market. It's so powerful that the federal government has endorsed it through law in the form of what's called automatic enrollment. Companies will automatically enroll participants in the plan, pick the investments, and hope the employee, after being notified of the action, of course, will not notice the funds being gone, and will live on the net paycheck. And it works! This is a good thing. It helps people save money and retire one day by accumulating a balance in an account they can live on rather than forcing them to fight their propensity to spend each and every month for their entire working lives.

The same goes for life insurance. To sign up for FEGLI requires one form and the naming of a beneficiary. Whatever arrives in the paycheck after the premium is deducted is yours to live on. To buy private life insurance requires a few more steps, however could include working with an advisor that will usually be part of a comprehensive financial plan that calculates the need, facilitates the coverage and acts as an advocate in the marketplace therefore providing significant piece of mind in the process.

So how much life insurance do you need? The answers to this question have ranged from a basic multiplier to entire books. The multiplier concept says that you take your annual income and multiply it times a factor based on your age. The factors will vary depending on the source, with "just invest the money and you'll be fine" types being on the low end, and large multiples of salary on the high end.

One example might be to take a 20x multiple if you are under 40, a 15x multiple if you are between 40 and 50, 10x multiple from 50 to 60, and so on. So someone under 40 who earns $50,000 would multiply the income by 20 to get a $1 million life insurance need. This system can be too simplistic, and doesn't take into account a household's particular financial situation, but if you don't have any life insurance and this calculation motivates you to go buy a $1 million policy, go ahead and use it. Your family will thank you.

Alternatively, a person can consider how life would look if his or her spouse wasn't around any longer. Did the person work? If so, how much of that income needs to be replaced? Will the surviving spouse work? If so, should child daycare costs come out of the insurance proceeds or will the surviving spouse be able to earn enough to cover it without additional funds? Is there a mortgage on the property? If so, should it, and possibly other personal debts like car loans, be paid off to limit the monthly expenses of the survivor?

How about paying for college? A calculation would need to be performed to project out the future cost of college for all of the children, regardless of the time frame involved and the unknown growth rate of college costs over that period. Are there any organizations or causes each spouse would like to see funded by some of the life insurance proceeds? What if there isn't such an organization preferred right now but there might be one later, if the person ends up getting sick from a certain illness, or if he or she develops strong feelings about a cause years after the insurance coverage is purchased?

What about estate taxes? The family could accumulate enough assets over the years of owning the policy to incur estate tax upon death, and who knows what Congress will set the estate tax limit at in the future? In fact, the policy itself, depending on how it's owned, could cause the family to exceed whatever threshold Congress may set. These unknown variables explain why some in the industry come up with handy simplistic formulas like those mentioned earlier.

What it comes down to is an honest conversation between the family and a trusted insurance advisor or financial planner. I have never had a beneficiary turn a death benefit check away because it's too large. I have also never had a beneficiary who wouldn't trade those funds back in for the loved one who died. Take a look at the budget to discuss affordability, and consider the debts and future debts such as college that should be paid for with the proceeds. Then look at household income and calculate how much income would be lost if the insured passed away and how long they realistically would have worked.

It's been said that when you retire that your need for life insurance goes away, but is that true? The best way to answer this question is to ask yourself whether the goals and uses of the proceeds from a life insurance policy have become any less valuable to you. Now that you have reached retirement, has it become less important to you to see that your children, or your likely grandchildren, go to college? Has it become less important that no matter how long you enjoy your retirement, or how much of your assets you spend during that time, there's still assets you can pass on to your family or an organization?

How about ensuring that the pension you earned isn't lost forever when you and your spouse pass away? If you're in retirement, and life has settled down a little bit finally, you will probably come to the conclusion that these goals have become more important, not less. So how do you make sure the assets you worked so hard to accumulate are sufficient to provide for your lifestyle throughout retirement but also leave some left over?

Well, you can limit spending, but this may not be an option because of the increased cost of living, health care costs, and possibly long-term care costs. This is in addition to the fact that retirement is supposed to be the long-awaited opportunity to spend your assets on enjoyable products and experiences, not a time to avoid doing so for the sake of the children and grandchildren. Well, at least not for the children!

Another option would be to take additional risk with your investments, seeking growth beyond what is necessary to draw on them for retirement, thereby ensuring the principal remains. However, what happens if the markets don't cooperate? What if your tolerance and interest in the markets winds down as you age to the point where this isn't a strategy that allows you to sleep at night?

Permanent life insurance can guarantee income tax-free cash to the precise people to whom you wish it to go, at the precise moment it needs to, in the exact amount you choose. The cost to ensure this legacy can be budgeted for through income planning and can be kept to a fixed amount throughout retirement regardless of how other expenses change over time.

Whether you work in the private sector or work for the government, all the following types of insurance are available to you. The best policy for you depends on your goals, your budget, and your personal preferences.

Term Life

Term life insurance is the most basic of coverage. You pay a premium that doesn't change over the term of the policy, and if the insured dies, the death benefit will be paid to the policy's beneficiary. The term can be anywhere from five to thirty years, with some unique contracts even lasting longer. Term insurance is easy to understand and usually obtained by people with a long working career ahead of them, because it's the cheapest form of insurance and a large amount of coverage can be secured. As one gets older, term insurance is less accessible. The whole reason a life insurance company can offer a 10-year term policy to 55-year-olds cheaply for the remainder of their working career is because it's statistically unlikely they will die during that 10-year period. Offering a 10-year term policy to a 65-year-old, or a 30-year term policy to a 55-year–old, for example, is a whole different story.

So what happens at the end of the term? If you have a term life insurance contract and you look at one of the first pages, it will have a schedule of premiums. Over the initial term of the contract, the premium is as you might expect, but you will see in most cases that after that, the premium becomes extraordinarily high, and increases annually. This feature is called renewability. The owner of the policy is welcome to keep the policy as long as they would like, but the premium is only fixed for the initial term. So why would anyone pay this higher premium? Let's say the insured was in fine health when the policy was bought and maybe even got a favorable health rating. But by year 18 of the 20-year term, something was wrong with the person's health. And by the end of the term, the insured was diagnosed as terminal. What a heartbreaking scenario for a family to have coverage for 20 years, and as soon as it ends the insured dies and the family receives nothing. This outcome can be avoided by paying the premium in year 21 and then collecting the death benefit when the insured passes away.

An alternative to renewing the policy on an annual basis with a rapidly increasing premium is to convert the contract. Conversion is a powerful planning tool as long as the policy owner is aware of the option and considers its advantages. Term policies are a specified number of years, such as 20 years, but, for example, a given contract may be converted into a permanent policy any time prior to the end of the fifteenth contract year without having to show evidence of insurability.

The important aspect of conversion is evidence of insurability. When the contract was originally taken out, the insured may have been young, active, and not requiring any prescription drugs. Fifteen years later, however, it may be different. If the person's health isn't quite the same due to weight gain, diabetes, high blood pressure, or any other ailment, then he or she can maintain the great rating they received at the beginning of the term. You have to be aware of the end of the conversion period, however, because it's not necessarily the end of the normal term period. Work with a financial planner to interpret your contract and make sure you have this discussion well before the end of the term so that you have time to discuss your goals and the cost of permanent protection.

Within the marketplace of permanent protection there are actually several options that allow customization of the relationship the owner is looking to have with the policy. The premiums may be structured to guarantee coverage or just assumed to carry the policy out to a specified age based on performance of a particular asset. Even further that asset may be a market index such as stocks or bonds, or a fixed interest-based environment or a combination of the two. Here are some specific types of coverage and their advantages and disadvantages.

Whole Life

Whole life is the old-fashioned insurance that lasts for the entirety of life and has been around a long time as an option to consumers. This is guaranteed coverage and may allow the insured to participate in dividends from the insurance company. The coverage is guaranteed, but the dividends are not. Whole life isn't used as much as in the past due to the greater perceived opportunity offered by products that allow participation in the securities markets that have grown over the last few decades.

The premiums for whole life will generally be the most expensive per increment of coverage in the market today, but they provide a correspondingly greater peace of mind. The owner will know that coverage is guaranteed, will see an increase over time in the cash value, and depending on the performance of this cash value may even be able to stop paying premiums while the coverage remains intact.

Universal Life

This form of insurance is still designed to be permanent, or for the entire life of the insured, but how it gets there is different. Cash value may build up over time due to premiums by the owner and interest credits the cash value earns over time. Simultaneously, the insurance company annually pulls out the cost of insurance, the funds it requires to insure the individual for that year, and net cash value is settled each year.

In other words, as the cost of insurance increases with the age of the insured, it may be that the cash value increases with it, stays level, or decreases due to low interest rates. It's also possible that it will decrease due to the choice of the owner not to pay the full premium, or any premium at all. As cash value decreases, if the cost of insurance becomes too large for what's left, the policy will collapse. The coverage will end and, barring increased and immediate premiums paid by the owner, the contract will be over. This may seem unfair, but it's the nature of this type of contract. The opposite scenario is possible, too, where interest rates rise, causing the cash value to grow faster than originally forecasted. Also, some contracts these days will include provisions that guarantee the death benefit to certain ages such as life expectancy or age 100, regardless of the cash value performance. The key is to monitor the progress of the policy over time through what's called an in-force illustration. It can be ordered directly from the insurance company, and various assumptions can be used to assess the strength of the policy. The insurance agent, or any insurance advisor interested in providing you good service, can assist in this forecasting process.

Variable Life/Variable Universal Life

The financial services industry came a long way when it made this form of life insurance a security, which means it is an investment that can lose value but also comes with the market's potential. The concept is the same as universal life, where the cost of insurance is debited periodically and the cash value rises or falls separately. The difference is that it does so not with interest rates but with vehicles called subaccounts that invest in stocks and bonds similar to mutual funds.

The possible outcomes increase exponentially because varying returns in the investment markets are much higher than interest rate-based volatility and can include negative returns. Whether this coverage is best suited for a particular situation is a subject for a conversation with a good financial planner who deals with life insurance. It's important to understand the best, average, and worst-case scenarios given the chosen premium and diversified asset allocation established in the policy.

SUL (Survivorship Universal Life)

Survivorship Universal Life isn't used as often as the opportunity for it comes up. This type of insurance insures two lives with one policy and pays out a death benefit at the passing of the last insured.

At the passing of the first insured the contract continues in force and premiums remain due. Usually an SUL contract is employed when estate tax is expected at the death of the last spouse. For example, if a family has calculated their net worth and other than gifting, alternative techniques, or changes in the estate tax limit, they expect to owe approximately $500,000 they have two options.

Their estate can either sell assets upon settlement to pay the tax, or they can secure a guaranteed benefit of the amount of the tax in exchange for a fixed annual premium. To structure the contract so the death benefit itself isn't included in the estate, an Irrevocable Life Insurance Trust (ILIT) is sometimes used. See an estate attorney to understand this form of estate planning and how it may assist the overall plan.

SUL can be a powerful planning tool because, provided the goal is to leave assets to beneficiaries, a larger amount of tax-free dollars can be structured for the same premium. For example, a husband and wife have been married for more than 30 years and know each other so well that they finish each other's thoughts. They have three children and eight grandchildren. The house has long ago been paid for, and their assets and pensions cover their living expenses. They've run the numbers, and if either one of them passed away, the survivor would be fine from an income standpoint.

So now they are interested in maximizing their estate for their children through life insurance because of its guarantees and tax-free status. The problem is that the husband isn't in the best health and may not be insurable. If he could get coverage and then does pass away prior to his wife, she inherits assets she doesn't need and they become part of her estate, possibly subjecting them to estate tax at her death. With a survivorship universal life policy, they can increase the amount of the death benefit, make it available at the appropriate time, lower the cost, and depending on the ownership keep it out of both of their estates.

Life insurance is not the consumer's favorite subject. It's also not the easiest to understand given the increased complexity of the industry, as one can see from the various types explained here. It's all about goals. What do you want your money to do and what are the pitfalls that could stop you from accomplishing those goals? If doing the right thing financially, or providing for your loved ones, is a goal, then life insurance has to be part of the conversation.

8
CHAPTER

Job Security, Wages, Leave, and Other Benefits

Peter was a hard worker. All he ever knew was working as an engineer for a contractor on office building contracts. It paid well enough to support his family when combined with the salary his wife earned as a teacher.

This chapter covers a variety of other miscellaneous benefits offered through the federal government and some private-sector employers. The intent is to show how what may seem like small human resource functions can actually prove to be valuable benefits both financially and personally.

Peter had been doing the same job for 15 years now, and if he could just hold on for another 20 or so they'd get the house paid off, put the children through school, and maybe accumulate a little bit to spend once they retired. It wasn't a complicated plan, which meant it was a perfect fit for him. He just wanted to go to work each day, spend time with his family when he could, and keep life simple.

One day Peter started to feel something in his feet. He couldn't really describe what it was, but it felt like they started to get heavy independently of the rest of his body. It took a couple of months for him to get to a doctor. After several appointments and tests, it took some time for the doctor to figure out what was going on. Each time Peter went in for a test he got a little more nervous. Then one day his whole life changed: His doctor said, "You have muscular dystrophy."

He felt like he couldn't breathe when he heard the news. Questions raced through his mind. "What do I do now? When will it go away? Does it ever go away? What if it gets worse and I can't do my job?"

As the years passed, Peter and his wife figured out ways to cope, and they were fortunate in that they had good health insurance. Eventually, however, his condition got bad enough to prevent him from doing his job. They tried to make ends meet, but it was just too difficult.

There was one employee benefit the company didn't offer. It turned out to be the one he could have used the most; disability insurance.

"I just never realized I needed to go out and find insurance to protect against the possibility I couldn't do my job. I worked hard, tried to stay healthy, I wouldn't even have known where to start to get that coverage," Peter said.

Peter's retirement plan didn't work out how he had envisioned it. With help from family and organizations like the Muscular Dystrophy Association, they were able to put in place certain routines that made life manageable. Unfortunately they ended up losing the house and had to lean on some of those family members for a place to live.

The children went to college, but they had to take out student loans to cover tuition and expenses.

Disability is just one of the many miscellaneous events and possible employee benefits that require a major financial planning decision over the course of someone's career. Other things such as leave to ensure mental health, college savings plans through payroll deduction to put money away for school, performance reviews, and an organized corporate structure to maintain worker motivation over a period of decades all add up to keeping an employee focused on the company's goals and seeing their own goals progressing.

When you work for the federal government, there are so many of these various benefits that periodic workshops are offered just to learn about them all.

Before we look at some of them, though, let's consider the cost of benefits.

Cost of Benefits

According to a Congressional Budget Office (CBO) study that came out in January 2012, the benefits provided to federal civilian employees cost 48% more than those provided to private-sector workers. This same study found that across all income levels the average federal civilian employee earns 2% more than their private-sector counterpart. It outlined that those with only a high school diploma averaged 21% more, while those with advanced degrees earned less than their equivalents in the private sector.

In the following sections, we'll take a look at the federal provisions for the following benefits and look at some recent rulings:

- Job Stability
- GS pay system
- Leave programs
- Federal Student Loan Repayment Program
- Disability Income
- Annuity for minor children
- Employer-sponsored seminars on retirement and Employee assistance programs

Job Stability

Among the average workers across all industries who started their job between the ages of 39 and 44, 68% had moved on to another position by the end of the fifth year, according to a Bureau of Labor Statistics study done in 2010. In today's fast-paced economy, workers feel the need to move on to new opportunities, or the company makes the decision for them with increasingly sudden restructuring events or profitability downturns that eliminate jobs. By comparison, a CBO study in 2007 showed that a given federal worker had been employed for 16.5 years on average as of 2005, which was the most recent year the study included. So in general, a federal employee had been in a consistent level of employment for three times the length of someone in the private sector.

GS (General Schedule) System

Pay over the course of one's tenure while working for the federal government usually falls within the GS (General Schedule) system. This system is an organized, lifelong opportunity to work one's way up the ladder and to earn greater income. It consists of 15 grades and 10 steps inside each grade, and pay within each step of each grade is determined by Congress and the president annually.

Advancements up each step or grade are rewarded due to tenure and acceptable performance. Waiting periods exist to ensure that tenure plays a role in one's ability to move up to higher levels. Employees must wait one year to reach levels 2, 3, or 4, and they must wait two years for levels 5, 6, or 7. Finally, three years is required for steps 8, 9, and 10. This may seem like an arbitrary employee advancement system, but think of it from the perspective of a typical small business or an informally run company where advancement is based on profitability and rare opportunities for additional responsibility.

Most people really just want a job they can arrive to, get their work done, and focus their life's work on other goals. They work hard, respect their employers, and maybe even really enjoy their day-to-day activities. The existence of this grade-and-step system allows the employee to enjoy consistency of employment and even perhaps a vision for growth that can be seen decades ahead of time.

Leave

There are several different forms of leave that are accrued over time. However the main ones are sick leave and annual leave. This depends on the nature of the federal employment, reason for the need for leave, or the award given that includes additional time off, among others.

Annual leave is given automatically at the inception of employment and only requires approval by the supervisor to take. For employees with less than three years of service, a four-hour period, or half day, is earned for each biweekly pay period. Once three years is achieved, but less than 15 years, a six-hour period is available for each pay period. Finally, those with 15 years of service a day is available for each pay period that goes by.

Annual leave can be stored over time, with a maximum of 30 days that can be rolled over and, upon retirement, be received as a one-time lump sum payment in lieu of taking the leave. This is a taxable distribution, but may amount to a rather large sum depending on the tenure of the worker and comes at an opportune time in one's life.

Many clients will use these funds to wrap up loose ends in their finances, which can put them across the finish line of the necessary steps before retirement. They may pay off the last of the mortgage, or some outstanding debts they had accumulated near the end of their working career, including fixing up the house or getting the children through the final years of advanced schooling.

Wiping out monthly expenses like this sometimes makes the difference between negative cash flow and being able to retire. Others over the years have used these funds to finally take that long around-the-world trip they've been working so hard to obtain.

The following are websites devoted entirely to explaining and maintaining information about federal employee news, benefits, and employment opportunities:

http://www.opm.gov
http://www.usa.gov

These sites provide a wealth of information and allow the comprehensive benefits discussed here in this book to be tracked by employees and their families. Health insurance, leave, pay, retirement, disability, and current events are catalogued in an easy-to-use format. Although I would caution that it is not always the most up to date so review the information thoroughly.

Federal Student Loan Repayment Program

The Federal Student Loan Repayment Program exists as a recruitment tool used by federal agencies to attract highly qualified employees for federal employment. For example, if a private-sector employee achieved an advanced degree or highly specialized degree using a federally insured student loan and accumulated $30,000 of debt in the process, the federal government can, in addition to all the other employee benefits available to the person, offer to repay up to $10,000 annually and $60,000 in total of the prospective employee's debt.

The payments may not be made directly to the employee and must go directly to the loan holder, and payments have to be for an existing loan, not an arrangement where the employee goes out and specifically obtains the degree under the agreement that it will be covered. However, having $30,000 plus interest of monthly loan repayment expenses entirely covered while obtaining a secure position can be a life-changer. The employee must sign and meet a three year contract to receive this benefit.

Disability Income

The story of Peter related a health event that restricted him from earning a living, and such occurrences can have devastating consequences for a household. To plan for this possibility, people are encouraged to purchase disability insurance.

Disability insurance is a contract with an insurance company that pays a monthly benefit for a specified period of time if a person meets the definition of disability stated in the contract.

There are varying definitions of one's inabilities depending on how comprehensive a policy the insured qualifies for and how much they want to spend.

For example, let's say a surgeon has an accident and can no longer perform the lucrative activity of surgery but could still teach or consult on potential surgeries for compensation. If the policy paid benefits under that circumstance, it would generally be referred to as an "Own Occupation" policy. In other words, benefits are payable because he or she can't perform their own occupation.

Alternatively, for a lower cost the policy could be referred to as an "Any Occupation" policy, and in this same scenario the surgeon would not receive anything from the policy because of his ability to still earn a living consulting, even if it's a much lower-paying one. In the event of a health diagnosis that prevented the person from performing any meaningful task that paid wages, then the policy would kick in.

It's possible to have a type of policy that initially would not pay out benefits, but later, as the condition worsened, would begin to do. This is where a good insurance advisor is invaluable in the financial planning process. Such an advisor can help you to not only understand which type of policy is best from a budget perspective but to also manage the claim process to assure the insured that he or she receives everything the policy has promised to pay out.

A typical policy with these benefits for a healthy career-oriented individual can cost in the range of $5,000 annually, although the cost will vary widely depending on the age, health, policy features, and income level of the insured. CSRS and FERS employees who hold enough tenure actually have the additional benefit of disability insurance built into their pension calculations, which saves them thousands of dollars a year in insurance premiums. In other words, if you qualify your pension will begin if you become disabled. The qualification requirements for FERS and CSRS employees are similar, with FERS members needing 18 months of employment and CSRS members needing five years of service. Under both CSRS and FERS, the condition must be expected to last at least one year. This is meant as a summary as the eligibility requirements can be more complicated. A summary of them is listed here:

> http://www.opm.gov/retire/pre/fers/disability.asp#Computation.

Both types use a definition of disability that states that the worker must not be able to perform their occupation or a similar one of their grade level across all agencies within their metropolitan area. Once it is determined that a disability is present and expected to continue, regardless of age, a percentage of their salary becomes payable for the entirety of the remaining working years, provided the disability continues. For both CSRS and FERS employees, it is 40% of the highest three years' average earnings and is payable until full retirement age. There are some adjustments to this formula in the first year and upon reaching age 62, available at the URL listed above. CSRS employees are not entitled to Social Security, so they cannot qualify for additional disability income, but FERS employees can. Any benefit Social Security approves, however, reduces the amount of the pension income they receive by 60% of what Social Security pays out. Receiving 40% may not seem like much, but if someone's earning $100,000 a year and it all goes to nothing out of the blue at age 45, still being able to collect $40,000 for the next 17 years, or $680,000, could be the difference between a manageable life and total financial catastrophe.

Survivor Benefit for Minor or Disabled Children

Minor children of an employee who passes away while employed (or who is already retired) may benefit from a program that pays out annuity income to each of them until they reach age 18, or age 22 if a full-time student. A child who is disabled prior to the age of 18 will continue to receive this benefit for the duration of his or her lifetime as long as they remain disabled. The amount each child receives depends on how many children qualify, and the marital status of the parents. For children of FERS employees and retirees, the amount is reduced by any income the minor child receives from Social Security, which offers a similar benefit.

Employer-Sponsored Seminars on Retirement and Employee Assistance Programs

Given the comprehensive, and many times complicated, nature of the various benefits offered to federal government workers, seminars are offered periodically specifically to outline their features. These may be short workshops or seminars on pension analysis that take the entire day and are held during the work week. Take advantage of these events, because they are opportunities to ask questions, run scenarios, and hear the latest adjustments to calculations that have occurred. And it's a day away from work!

Recent Rulings

If it seemed so far like the benefits are about as good as it gets, then recent legislative rulings over the past several years make them even better. In 2004, the Federal Workforce Flexibility Act was passed, which among other things expanded the accrual rate of annual leave for executive, scientific, and professional workers to the current levels listed earlier.

Prior to this, the accrual was lower. Additionally, the 2004 law reviewed and enhanced training programs for existing employees, established a new form of compensatory time off for work-related travel, and enhanced the ability of agencies to pay bonuses as a recruitment tool. Additionally, in the National Defense Authorization Act of 2010 was a provision referred to as the "Reemployment of Civilian Retirees to Meet Exceptional Employment Needs." This provision allowed agencies to designate certain individuals as highly skilled and allow them to retire to begin receiving federal retirement benefits such as their pension, and go back to work in their previous position. The amount of work is limited to part time, 1,040 hours annually, and for a maximum of 3,120 hours.

All of these benefit opportunities create an environment of stability and consistency in the financial planning process. A family looking to accomplish several substantial financial goals over a period of decades requires patience and long-term thinking. Just as important, it requires safety nets against the unfortunate pitfalls of life. Health circumstances, accidents, house repairs, learning disabilities, and so on negatively affect the steady progress made by a family in planning its financial future. A financial planner is tasked with recognizing these obstacles and putting the protections in place to first solidify what has already been accomplished and then create a road map for future growth. When guaranteed retirement income, disability and health insurance, job security, training opportunities, investment accumulation accounts, and life and long-term care insurance are already in place, the foundation is there to accomplish anything.

What to Do for the Rest of Us

Some of these benefits may be similar to those offered by a private-sector employer, especially the larger ones. The important point is to track them and see how they affect your family's planning and goals. Meet with your human resources contact and ask for a full breakdown of what benefits are available. Take that to your financial planner and ask how they can be used to their maximum potential. You may save money by adding valuable insurance protection you didn't know you could without a burdensome cost.

CHAPTER 9

Working Toward Your Goals

All the stories presented in this book are fictitious scenarios of events that play out with similar details in financial planners' offices across the country every day.

Many people go through life making financial decisions on their own using the best intentions and the information available to them. Sometimes they succeed in their endeavors and sometimes they don't. The concern is that as the investment markets become even more complex and global in nature, efficient diversification becomes more important. With the government's need for additional revenues, growing tax efficiency becomes more complicated. And as protection from risk grows more expansive due to the variety of insurance coverages necessary, going it alone seems almost impossible. Thus we've seen the meteoric growth of the individual financial planning and wealth management industry.

This chapter outlines what to expect from working with a financial planner. Regardless of your employment status, you will have goals. Write those goals down and bring them in along with your questions when you meet with your financial planner.

Comprehensive financial planners will be familiar with all the topics discussed here—and more. They will educate you on the various options available and collaborate with you about your preferences as they help you to create a plan of action. The following are 10 absolute requirements when working with a planner. Being prepared will make you more comfortable and help you get more out of the process.

1. **Personal Rapport**—When you meet with someone who offers to help you, you may hear some big promises. You are discussing one of the important possessions in your life, your money, so you had better like and trust the person. And make sure your spouse likes the person, too, because the three of you make a team and there needs to be comfort in the decisions being made.

   During the initial appointment, the financial planner should listen to your concerns, allow you to ask questions, and give you confidence that he or she is a highly competent professional. And your situation should not be something the planner has never encountered before.

2. **Know yourself**—Just as important as trusting the arrangements your planner is proposing for you is knowing yourself and what you really want to accomplish.

   During the initial meetings the planner will ask you questions about your likes and dislikes, your previous experiences with financial decision making, and what you want to accomplish (in many cases five, fifteen, or even twenty years from now). It can be difficult to know these answers off the top of your head, but that's all right. It isn't, however, a reason to put off the meeting or to procrastinate indefinitely, as many people do. Keep attending the meetings and talking it through with your spouse. You'll be surprised how much you get accomplished and how motivating the process becomes.

3. **Look for credentials** — This is a step generally done prior to meeting with a potential candidate. Financial planners come in all shapes and sizes. Calling oneself a financial planner only requires basic licensing. Being good at it is a different story. They have to be able to explain technical facts in a way that a lay person can understand. They have to turn an emotional decision into a logical one. As it relates to the knowledge necessary to make suitable recommendations, though, it's helpful for a planner to have one or more of a few credentials to document commitment to their own education process, and have undergone training relevant to the discussions that you are having with the planner.

   One of the main credentials for financial planners is the CFP designation. This stands for Certified Financial Planner and is provided by the CFP Board of Standards in Washington, D.C. Applicants are required to pass a comprehensive exam, hold a bachelor's degree, achieve a level of experience within the industry, and act as a fiduciary on their client's behalf. Other options for planners are the CLU and ChFC designations. These stand for Chartered Life Underwriter and Chartered Financial Consultant, respectively, and also require documented experience and the successful completion of a series of exams related to insurance, estate planning, and general financial planning concepts.

   The list of professional designations available for planners to earn has grown rapidly over the years, and not all of them are worth mentioning. If you stick with individuals who have one or more of the designations mentioned here, and perhaps commonly accepted levels of expertise like a master's degree, CPA, or license to practice law, you should be on the right track to working with someone devoted to the craft of financial planning.

4. **Bring your documentation** — Whether the initial appointment takes place at your home or the planner's office, there is going to be an exchange of information. If the appointment is worth having, it's worth bringing your data. This should include your investment account statements, employee benefits handbook, the previous year's tax return, life insurance and annuity contracts, stocks or bond certificates, pension and Social Security benefit statements, and any other documents you feel relevant. The more data the better.

   If there is a concern about privacy or trust of the planner, then pull the documents together and hold them until you're ready. Perhaps black out the account numbers. But sooner or later the process will require them, and you'll feel better that you're ready to hit the ground running.

5. **Tell the financial planner your concerns and ask questions** — Effective communication is the biggest challenge in a successful financial planning relationship. It's normal to have concerns and questions. What can cause problems is if they are not immediately discussed. Feel free to express concerns about how much risk you're taking, or to bring up an article you find that talks about investment strategies, or to request that the financial planner restate a concept already explained in the previous meeting that needs to be discussed again. These are all a helpful part of the process, one that the planner should enthusiastically welcome.

6. **Meet regularly** — In the initial stages there's obviously going to be regular meetings. Perhaps every week until the plan is fully put in place. However, that's not where the process

should end. At the very least an annual review should be taking place to assess changes to your situation and to check the progress toward your goals. If periodic meetings aren't occurring, or at least welcomed, that's a big red flag that indicates something is amiss in the relationship.

7. **Know the fees** — Financial planners are in business to help their clients, and they do their work in a manner that allows them to earn a living. These fees will come in a variety of forms. Some planners will charge a onetime fee to complete a comprehensive financial plan. They will make non-binding recommendations to you regarding your overall situation and offer to implement those recommendations on your behalf. Some of the implementation may result in a commission or the use of a product. In other cases, there's fee-based asset management.

For example, if you invest $100,000 in a diversified portfolio of mutual funds and ETFs and the planner charges 1% or $1,000 annually for his or her services, you know exactly what you are paying and the planner is encouraged to provide stability to your portfolio while achieving growth over time because it will cause the fee you pay to grow.

Some planners will use mutual fund accounts to invest on their client's behalf, and these may come with what's referred to as a load. This load will either be a percentage of the initial deposit or a contingent load that only kicks in if the fund is sold within a certain period of time after purchase. Other products, such as insurance policies and annuities, provide a commission to the agent offering the contract. None of these arrangements is inherently better than another. It's what makes the client most comfortable, so listen to the planner's proposals and decide accordingly.

8. **Get some coverage** — According to LIMRA's 2011 Life Insurance Ownership Study, only one-third of Americans

are covered by individual life insurance, which is the lowest level in fifty years. The financial planning community wants to change that, and not just to sell you insurance policies to earn a commission. It's to ensure that families are protected.

Therefore, if you're working with a good planner, it's likely you will be presented with the protections provided by a life, disability, or long-term care insurance policy. Unfortunately, these policies are not free. But just like the stories we read earlier in the life insurance and LTC chapters, things can happen. No one thinks it will happen to them. It's human nature. If you go through a planning process and it's uncovered that some form of coverage is suitable, and the planner shows how to pay for it, consider it an investment in peace of mind.

9. **Discuss income** — The most popular topic when working with someone is talking about retirement. "When can I stop depriving myself of all this money I'm earning and start enjoying it? Even more so, when can I stop caring about all these employee benefits my company is giving me and focus on the grandchildren, my hobbies, and traveling?" And so income planning has grown as a specialty and arranges assets in a way that produces reliable income streams that last one's lifetime. A pile of money, no matter how large, isn't that valuable if there isn't a plan to live off it for an extended period of time. Here's where the goals come into play again. In retirement, is the wish to preserve the corpus of what you worked so hard to accumulate and to pass it on to your children? If so, the income it can provide may be lower. Alternatively, would you like to spend the assets down to enjoy retirement to its fullest, allowing the children to learn how to accumulate their own wealth?

10. **Know the lingo** — Investment management uses terminology to describe diversification of assets to preserve and

grow wealth. It can get complicated. Even the types of accounts that hold this wealth come in a variety of forms, such as IRA, Roth IRA, SEP IRA, Keogh, Trust, TOD, and so on. Within asset allocation, specifically, are terms like beta, alpha, standard deviation, and Monte Carlo simulation (not the sandwich). Entire books can be, and have been; written on these functions of investing, but a lack of knowledge about how they work doesn't need to throw off the whole process. They are meant simply to provide parameters for the environment in which your assets will be invested. Beta and correlation, in general, measures how much the movements of your portfolio occur in relation to the market as a whole. Alpha tries to measure performance against a benchmark, and standard deviation outlines, statistically, the likely possible returns of a given portfolio over a specified period of time. This is not to say the returns can't fall out of this possible range, as 2008 revealed. The key is to ask questions, understand the risk, and not take more than you can handle, diversify, and track. It sounds like a great deal of work? It is. That's where a good financial planner comes in.

The goal of this book was to show you, the federal employee, that the wealth of benefits that comes from your hard earned efforts as civil servants creates tremendous opportunities for achieving your personal financial goals in collaboration with the right professionals.

Another goal was to show those in the private sector that you can still accomplish all you wish for your family and retirement using tools created in the marketplace and having good help.

Knowledge, along with good communication, is power. With a little hard work—and you're already off to an excellent start by reading this book—there's no limit to what you can accomplish!

Made in the USA
San Bernardino, CA
16 September 2014